AS/A-Level Student Text Guide
Andrew Green
Series Editor: Marian Cox
D0541834
The Whitsun Weddings
821.09
Philip Larkin
LITERATURE

Philip Allan Updates
Market Place
Deddington
Oxfordshire
OX15 0SE
Tel: 01869 338652
Fax: 01869 337590
e-mail: sales@philipallan.co.uk
www.philipallan.co.uk

ISBN-13: 978-1-84489-405-5
ISBN-10: 1-84489-405-3

Printed by MPG Books, Bodmin

Environmental information
The paper on which this title is printed is sourced from mills using wood from managed, sustainable forests.

P00472

Contents

Introduction
Aims of the guide ... 2
Assessment Objectives ... 2
Revision advice ... 3
Writing examination essays ... 5

Text Guidance
Contents
Biography ... 10
Women and marriage ... 14
Jazz ... 16
The Movement ... 18
The 1960s ... 20
Language ... 22
Themes ... 24
Imagery ... 33
Opposites ... 40
Humour ... 46
The key poems
'Here' ... 47
'Mr Bleaney' ... 50
'The Whitsun Weddings' ... 52
'Dockery and Son' ... 57
'An Arundel Tomb' ... 60
Notes on the other poems ... 65
Extracts from *Jill* and *A Girl in Winter* ... 72
Quotations ... 74
Literary terms and concepts ... 78

Questions and Answers
Essay questions, specimen plans and notes ... 84
Sample essays ... 89
Using the critics ... 95
References and further study ... 96

Introduction

Aims of the guide

The purpose of this Student Text Guide to Philip Larkin's *The Whitsun Weddings* is to enable you to organise your thoughts and responses to the poems, to deepen your understanding of their key features and aspects, and to help you to address the particular requirements of examination questions in order to obtain the best possible grade. The edition of *The Whitsun Weddings* used in preparing this guide is the one published by Faber and Faber in 1964. Reference is also made to *High Windows* (Faber and Faber, 1974), to the *Collected Poems of Philip Larkin*, edited by Anthony Thwaite (Faber and Faber, 1988), and to *Required Writing: Miscellaneous Pieces 1955–82* (Faber and Faber, 1983).

It is assumed that you have read and studied *The Whitsun Weddings* already under the guidance of a teacher or lecturer. This is a revision guide, not an introduction, although some of its content provides background information and analysis of particular poems. It can be read in its entirety in one sitting, or it can be dipped into and used as a reference guide to specific and separate aspects of the poems.

The remainder of this Introduction consists of an outline of the Assessment Objectives; revision advice; and guidance on writing examination essays.

The Text Guidance section consists of a series of subsections which examine key aspects of the poetry including themes, imagery and analysis of specific poems. Emboldened terms within the Text Guidance section are glossed in 'literary terms and concepts' (pp. 78–81).

The final section, Questions and Answers, provides examples of essay titles, essay plans and examination essays, along with advice on how to make use of criticism on Larkin in your own writing.

Assessment Objectives

The Assessment Objectives (AOs) for A-level English Literature are common to all boards:

AO1	communicate clearly the knowledge, understanding and insight appropriate to literary study, using appropriate terminology and accurate and coherent written expression
AO2i	respond with knowledge and understanding to literary texts of different types and periods

AO2ii	respond with knowledge and understanding to literary texts of different types and periods, exploring and commenting on relationships and comparisons between literary texts
AO3	show detailed understanding of the ways in which writers' choices of form, structure and language shape meanings
AO4	articulate independent opinions and judgements, informed by different interpretations of literary texts by other readers
AO5i	show understanding of the contexts in which literary texts are written and understood
AO5ii	evaluate the significance of cultural, historical and other contextual influences on literary texts and study

This can be summarised as:

AO1	clarity of written communication
AO2	informed personal response in relation to time and genre (literary context)
AO3	the creative literary process (context of writing)
AO4	critical and interpretative response (context of reading)
AO5	evaluation of influences (cultural context)

It is essential that you pay close attention to the AOs, and their weighting, for the board for which you are entered. These are what the examiner will be looking for, and you must address them *directly* and *specifically*, in addition to proving general familiarity with and understanding of the text, and being able to present an argument clearly, relevantly and convincingly.

Remember that the examiners are seeking above all else evidence of an *informed personal response* to the text. A revision guide such as this can help you to understand the text and to form your own opinions, but it cannot replace your own ideas and responses as an individual reader.

Revision advice

For the examined units it is possible that either brief or more extensive revision will be necessary because the original study of the text took place some time previously. It is therefore useful to know how to go about revising and which tried and tested methods are considered the most successful for literature exams at all levels, from GCSE to degree finals.

Below is a guide on how not to do it — think of reasons why not in each case. **Don't**:

- leave it until the last minute
- assume you remember the text well enough and don't need to revise at all
- spend hours designing a beautiful revision schedule
- revise more than one text at the same time
- think you don't need to revise because it is an open-book exam
- decide in advance what you think the questions will be and revise only for those
- try to memorise particular essay plans
- reread texts randomly and aimlessly
- revise for longer than 2 hours in one sitting
- miss school lessons in order to work alone at home
- try to learn a whole ring binder's worth of work
- rely on a study guide instead of the text

There are no short-cuts to effective exam revision; the only one way to know a text well, and to know your way around it in an exam, is to have done the necessary studying. If you use the following method, in six easy stages, for both open- and closed-book revision, you will not only revisit and reassess all your previous work on the text in a manageable way but will be able to distil, organise and retain your knowledge. Don't try to do it all in one go: take regular breaks for refreshment and a change of scene.

(1) Between a month and a fortnight before the exam, depending on your schedule (a simple list of stages with dates displayed in your room, not a work of art!), you will need to reread the text, this time taking stock of all your underlinings and marginal annotations as well. As you read, collect onto sheets of A4 the essential ideas and quotations as you come across them. The acts of selecting key material and recording it as notes are natural ways of stimulating thought and aiding memory.

(2) Reread the highlighted areas and marginal annotations in your critical extracts and background handouts, and add anything useful from them to your list of notes and quotations. Then reread your previous essays and the teacher's comments. As you look back through essays written earlier in the course, you should have the pleasant sensation of realising that you can now write much better on the text than you could then. You will discover that much of your huge file of notes is redundant or repeated, and that you have changed your mind about some beliefs, so that the distillation process is not too daunting. Selecting what is important is the way to crystallise your knowledge and understanding.

(3) During the run-up to the exam you need to do lots of practice essay plans to help you identify any gaps in your knowledge and give you practice in planning in 5–8 minutes. Past paper titles for you to plan are provided in this guide, some of which can be done as full timed essays — and marked strictly according to exam criteria — and will show whether length and timing are problematic for you. If you have not seen a copy of a real exam paper before you take your first module, ask to see a past paper so that you are familiar with the layout and rubric.

(4) About a week before the exam, reduce your two or three sides of A4 notes to a double-sided postcard of very small, dense writing. Collect a group of keywords by once again selecting and condensing, and use abbreviations for quotations (first and last word), and character and place names (initials). For the comparison unit your postcard will need to refer to key points, themes and quotations in both texts relevant to the specific theme or genre topic. The act of choosing and writing out the short quotations will help you to focus on the essential issues, and to recall them quickly in the exam. Make sure that your selection covers the main themes and includes examples of symbolism, style, comments on character, examples of irony, point of view or other significant aspects of the text. Previous class discussion and essay writing will have indicated which quotations are useful for almost any title; pick those which can serve more than one purpose, for instance those that reveal character and theme, and are also an example of language. In this way a minimum number of quotations can have maximum application.

(5) You now have in a compact, accessible form all the material for any possible essay title. There are only half a dozen themes relevant to a literary text so if you have covered these, you should not meet with any nasty surprises when you read the exam questions. You don't need to refer to your file of paperwork again, or even to the text. For the few days before the exam, you can read through your handy postcard whenever and wherever you get the opportunity. Each time you read it, which will only take a few minutes, you are reminding yourself of all the information you will be able to recall in the exam to adapt to the general title or to support an analysis of particular passages.

(6) A fresh, active mind works wonders, and information needs time to settle, so don't try to cram just before the exam. Relax the night before and get a good night's sleep. In this way you will be able to enter the exam room with all the confidence of a well-prepared candidate.

Writing examination essays

Essay content

One of the key skills you are being asked to demonstrate at A-level is the ability to select and tailor your knowledge of the text and its background to the question set in the exam paper. In order to reach the highest levels, you need to avoid 'pre-packaged' essays, which lack focus, relevance and coherence, and simply contain everything you know about the text. Be ruthless in rejecting irrelevant material, after considering whether it can be made relevant by a change of emphasis. Aim to cover the whole question, not just part of it; your response needs to demonstrate breadth and depth, covering the full range of text elements: character, event, theme and language. Only half a dozen approaches are possible for any set text, though they may be phrased in a variety of ways, and they are likely to refer to the key themes of the text. Preparation of the text therefore involves extensive discussion and practice at manipulating these core themes so that there should be no surprises in the exam. An apparently new angle is more likely to be something familiar presented in an unfamiliar way and you should not panic or reject the choice of question because you think you know nothing about it.

Exam titles are open-ended in the sense that there is not an obvious right answer, and you would therefore be unwise to give a dismissive, extreme or entirely one-sided response. The question would not have been set if the answer were not debatable. An ability and willingness to see both sides is an Assessment Objective and shows independence of judgement as a reader. Don't be afraid to explore the issues and don't try to tie the text into one neat interpretation. If there is ambiguity, it is likely to be deliberate on the part of the author and must be discussed; literary texts are complex and often paradoxical, and it would be a misreading of them to suggest that there is only one possible interpretation. You are not expected, however, to argue equally strongly or extensively for both sides of an argument, since personal opinion is an important factor. It is advisable to deal with the alternative view at the beginning of your response, and then construct your own view as the main part of the essay. This makes it less likely that you will appear to cancel out your own line of argument.

Choosing the right question

The first skill you must show when presented with the exam paper is the ability to choose the better, for you, of the two questions on your text where there is a choice. This is not to say that you should always go for the same type of essay (whole-text or poem-based), and if the question is not one with which you feel happy for any reason, you should seriously consider the other, even if it is not the type you normally prefer. It is unlikely but possible that a question contains a word you are not sure you know the meaning of, in which case it would be safer to choose the other one.

Don't be tempted to choose a question because of its similarity to one you have already done. Freshness and thinking on the spot usually produce a better product than attempted recall of a previous essay, which may have received only a mediocre mark in the first place. The exam question is unlikely to have exactly the same focus and your response may seem 'off centre' as a result, as well as stale and perfunctory in expression. Essay questions fall into the following categories: close section analysis and relation to whole text; characterisation; setting and atmosphere; structure and effectiveness; genre; language and style; themes and issues. Remember, however, that themes are relevant to all essays and that analysis, not just description, is always required.

Once you have decided which exam question to attempt, follow the procedure below for whole-text and passage-based, open- and closed-book essays.

(1) Underline all the key words in the question and note how many parts the question has.

(2) Plan your answer, using aspects of the key words and parts of the question as sub-headings, in addition to themes. Aim for 10–12 ideas. Check that the Assessment Objectives are covered.

(3) Support your argument by selecting the best examples of characters, events, imagery and quotations to prove your points. Remove ideas for which you can find no evidence.

(4) Structure your answer by grouping and numbering your points in a logical progression. Identify the best general point to keep for the conclusion.

(5) Introduce your essay with a short paragraph setting the context and defining the key words in the question as broadly, but relevantly, as possible.

(6) Write the rest of the essay, following your structured plan but adding extra material if it occurs to you. Paragraph your writing and consider expression, especially sentence structure and vocabulary choices, as you write. Signal changes in the direction of your argument with paragraph openers such as 'Furthermore' and 'However'. Use plenty of short, integrated quotations and use the words of the text rather than your own where possible. Use technical terms appropriately, and write concisely and precisely, avoiding vagueness and ambiguity.

(7) Your conclusion should sound conclusive and make it clear that you have answered the question. It should be an overview of the question and the text, not a repetition or a summary of points already made.

(8) Cross out your plan with a neat, diagonal line.

(9) Check your essay for content, style, clarity and accuracy. With neat crossings-out, correct errors of fact, spelling, grammar and punctuation. Improve expression if possible, and remove any repetition and irrelevance. Add clarification and missing evidence, if necessary, using omission marks or asterisks. Even at this stage, good new material can be added.

There is no such thing as a perfect or model essay; flawed essays can gain full marks. There is always something more which could have been said, and examiners realise that students have limitations when writing under pressure in timed conditions. You are not penalised for what you didn't say in comparison to some idealised concept of the answer, but rewarded for the knowledge and understanding you have shown. It is not as difficult as you may think to do well, provided that you are familiar with the text and have sufficient essay-writing experience. If you follow the above process and **underline, plan**, **support**, **structure**, **write** and **check**, you can't go far wrong.

Text Guidance

Contexts

Assessment Objective 5 requires the candidate to 'evaluate the significance of cultural, historical and other contextual influences on literary texts'. There are a number of contexts in which Larkin's *The Whitsun Weddings* can be viewed.

Biography

The poet, novelist and jazz critic Philip Arthur Larkin was born in Coventry on 9 August 1922. He was the only son and the younger child of Sidney and Eva Larkin. Sidney Larkin, a known Nazi sympathiser and admirer of Adolf Hitler, held the post of City Treasurer of Coventry from 1922 to 1944. As a boy Larkin was taken on holiday to Germany, which was by then firmly in the political grip of Nazism. He was taught by his father to admire the achievements of the German nation and, even as an adult, never truly escaped this influence. In 1941, in the face of the Nazi advance, when he was a student at Oxford and feared being called up to fight, Larkin would still not totally distance himself from and denounce Hitler. He observed in a letter to Jim Sutton:

> I expect Pop will be on the lookout for a secondhand copy of Norman Baynes's edition of Hitler's speeches. I looked into them and felt the familiar sinking of heart when I saw how *right* and yet how *wrong* everything had been. The disentanglement of this epoch will be a beautiful job for someone.

The influence of the father on the son is evident in terms of Larkin's character as well as his political views. Sidney Larkin was a highly intelligent but often intolerant man. He possessed a fine library and encouraged his son's bookish tendencies. The odd conditions of life in the Larkin household, where Sidney Larkin's narrow and misogynistic outlook was offset by an unexpected liberality on the subjects of reading and jazz music, no doubt contributed to the many contradictions that emerge in Larkin's subsequent life and writings. He was later to refer to his childhood as 'dull, pot-bound and slightly mad'. In fact, childhood and children remained anathemas to Larkin for the rest of his life. In 'The Savage Seventh', which appears in *Required Writing*, he observes:

> Until I began to meet grown-ups on more or less equal terms I fancied myself a kind of Ishmael. The realisation that it was not people I disliked but children was for me one of those celebrated moments of revelation.

From 1930 to 1940 Larkin attended the King Henry VIII School in Coventry, a boys' grammar school. He was a notoriously quiet and generally unremarkable student in his teachers' eyes, and his copious private writing (he had worked on four novels before he was 18) was largely unknown, except to a few close friends. As he went through the school, however, he began to make contributions to *The Coventrian*, the school magazine, which he coedited from 1939 to 1940.

Oxford years

On leaving school Larkin went up to St John's College, Oxford, again an all-male environment, where he met and developed close friendships with Kingsley Amis and Bruce Montgomery. These connections led to his involvement with what came to be known as the Movement, a group of young English writers, including Larkin, Amis, Donald Davie and Thom Gunn, that rejected the prevailing neo-Romantic trends in the English literary scene (see pp. 18–20). Owing to his poor eyesight, which meant he failed his army medical examination, Larkin was exempted from national service and was therefore able to complete his studies without interruption, gaining a first class honours degree in English. Larkin's educational background no doubt set him apart from many of his Oxford contemporaries, who would have attended public school, and created in him a sense of not belonging to any particular social group.

The love of jazz music Larkin had developed in Coventry grew into a passion in Oxford, and one he shared with his circle of friends. In his writing during this period he was influenced strongly by W. H. Auden, D. H. Lawrence and W. B. Yeats. The influence of Thomas Hardy, an author Larkin particularly admired, is evident in his ability to make the commonplace and often dreary elements of day-to-day existence the stuff of tough and uncompromising observation. Larkin's first nationally published poem, 'Ultimatum', appeared in *The Listener* on 28 November 1940.

Librarianship and writing

After graduation, Larkin returned to the family home, which was now in Warwick. He continued to write, spending much time on what was to be his first published novel, *Jill*. He attempted to gain employment in the civil service on two occasions, but failed both times, and eventually took a job as a librarian at Wellington in Shropshire, in November 1943. Full-time employment and part-time study to gain his qualifications as a librarian placed great demands on Larkin's time, but he continued to write and publish. He contributed a selection of early verse to the anthology *Poetry from Oxford in Wartime*, which appeared in 1945, and his first solo collection, *The North Ship*, was published in the same year. These were followed in 1946 by the publication of *Jill*. None of these works received a great deal of public or critical notice. *A Girl in Winter*, however, Larkin's second novel, which was completed in 1945 and published in 1947, attracted some acclaim.

In September 1946 Larkin took a post as assistant librarian at University College, Leicester. He continued his professional studies, becoming a member of the Library Association in 1949. During this period he completed a new collection of poems, entitled *In the Grip of Light*. This, however, was rejected. He moved jobs again in 1950, this time to Belfast, where he was sub-librarian at Queen's University, and began to write again. A small collection, *XX Poems*, was printed privately in 1951. Further poems appeared in pamphlets and a range of other publications, and were eventually gathered into a new collection, *The Less Deceived*, which was published in 1955. It was in this year that Larkin was appointed as librarian in the Brynmor Jones Library at the University of Hull (a post he held until 1985, the year of his death), overseeing the development of the library from a small collection in a ramshackle series of huts to a purpose-built facility with a staff and stock over six times larger than when he started the job.

The Whitsun Weddings, a collection of poems that won wide acclaim, appeared in 1964. This was followed in 1965 by recognition of Larkin's national (and international) standing as a poet in the award of the Queen's Gold Medal for Poetry. His continuing interest in jazz became more concrete at this time; from 1961 to 1971 he was the author of a series of monthly jazz record reviews for the *Daily Telegraph*. A collection of these was published by Faber and Faber as *All What Jazz: a Record Diary (1961–68)* in 1970 (a revised edition appeared in 1985). In 1973 Larkin edited the *Oxford Book of Twentieth Century Verse*. Then, in 1974, came the last of his own volumes of poetry, *High Windows*. By this time his composition of poetry had all but stopped; his last published poem, 'Aubade', appeared in the *Times Literary Supplement* in 1977.

Although there was no more poetry, other books did follow. *Required Writing: Miscellaneous Pieces 1955–82*, a collection of reviews and essays edited by Larkin's friend and literary executor Anthony Thwaite, came out in 1983. *Collected Poems 1938–83* was published after Larkin's death, in 1988. His correspondence appeared posthumously in 1992 as *Selected Letters of Philip Larkin, 1940–85*, and a volume of prose entitled *Further Requirements* was published in 2001, both again edited by Thwaite. Other recent additions to the canon of Larkin's work are *Larkin's Jazz: Essays and Reviews 1940–84*, a further collection of his jazz writings, and *Trouble at Willow Gables and Other Fictions* (edited by James Booth), a set of scurrilous tales that shed light on the author's sexuality.

Public honours and private life

Towards the end of his life, Larkin received a series of awards and honours, including the CBE in 1975. He was the chair of the Booker Prize committee in 1977, and in 1980 became an honorary fellow of the Library Association. In 1982 he was made a professor by the University of Hull, and in 1984 he was created a doctor of letters by the University of Oxford. On the death of his friend Sir John Betjeman he was offered the position of poet laureate, but declined, as he was no longer composing poetry. Ted Hughes accepted it instead. Shortly before he died he was awarded the Order of the Companion of Honour.

Profoundly influenced by his parents' unhappy marriage, Larkin remained unmarried and childless all his life. It is clear, however, that he was by no means sexually inactive, unlike the personas in a number of his poems (and especially the famous 'Annus Mirabilis' from *High Windows*). He was involved in long-term relationships with three women, the most significant of which was with Monica Jones, a professor of English, with whom he lived. His views on the states of marriage and singleness, and of children, form major **themes** within his literary oeuvre.

Like his father before him (a coincidence of which he was almost fatalistically aware), Larkin died of cancer of the oesophagus at the age of 63. The date of his death was 2 December 1985. He is buried in Cottingham Cemetery in Hull, and his minimalist epitaph reads: 'Philip Larkin 1922–1985 Writer'.

Key dates

1922 Born 9 August, second child and only son of Sidney and Eva Larkin.

1930 Attends King Henry VIII School, Coventry.

1933 Adolf Hitler and his Nazi Party seize power in Germany.

1939 Second World War begins following Hitler's invasion of Poland. Coedits *The Coventrian*, his school magazine.

1940 Goes up to Oxford, where he reads for a degree in English. There he meets Kinglsley Amis and Bruce Montgomery.

'Ultimatum', his first nationally published poem, appears in *The Listener.*

1943 Graduates with a first class honours degree in English. He is allowed to complete his degree and avoid military service because of his poor eyesight.

In November becomes a librarian at Wellington, Shropshire.

Meets Ruth Bowman, his first love.

1944 D-Day landings of Allied troops on the Normandy coast signal the beginning of the end of the Second World War.

1945 Contributes to *Poetry from Oxford in Wartime* and publishes *The North Ship*, his first collection of poetry.

Second World War ends. In its wake, 50 states from around the world create the United Nations.

1946 Publishes *Jill*, his first novel.

Becomes assistant librarian at University College, Leicester, where he meets Monica Jones.

1947 Publishes *A Girl in Winter*, his last completed novel.

1950 Becomes sub-librarian at Queen's University, Belfast.

1951 Privately publishes *XX Poems.*

1955 Publishes *The Less Deceived.*

Is appointed librarian at the Brynmor Jones Library, University of Hull.

Meets Maeve Brennan, later to become his third lover.

1957	The European Economic Community is formed in Rome.
1964	Publishes *The Whitsun Weddings.*
1965	Is awarded the Queen's Gold Medal for Poetry.
1969	Removal of British troops from East Suez.
1970	Publishes *All What Jazz: A Record Diary.*
1973	Edits the *Oxford Book of Twentieth Century Verse.*
1974	Publishes *High Windows.*
1975	Is awarded the CBE.
1977	'Aubade', his last published poem, appears in the *Times Literary Supplement.*
	Chairs the Booker Prize committee.
	Silver Jubilee of Queen Elizabeth II.
1979	Margaret Thatcher and her Conservative government come to power.
1983	Publishes *Required Writing: Miscellaneous Pieces 1955–82.*
1985	Dies 2 December of cancer of the oesophagus, aged 63.

Women and marriage

Larkin and women

Poems like 'High Windows' and 'Annus Mirabilis', from Larkin's 1974 collection *High Windows*, present the view of an inexperienced man who has missed the boat in terms of sex and the sexual liberation that began in the magical year of 1963. In reality, what these poems indicate is that public perceptions of sex, and the emotions of secrecy and guilt that formerly surrounded it, changed with the social revolutions of the 1960s. Larkin himself was certainly not sexually inexperienced. In 1945 he had sexual relations with Ruth Bowman, his first love and lover, and as the years progressed he was involved in long-term relationships with both Monica Jones (his lover for many years) and Maeve Brennan (who eventually became his lover in spite of her strong religious views). He also had an affair with Betty Mackereth, who worked in the library at the University of Hull.

This sexual activity would have come as a great surprise to Philip Brown, one of Larkin's contemporaries at Oxford and his roommate, who observed:

> Philip's sexuality was so obscured by his manner of approach and his general diffidence that frankly I would be surprised to hear that he had ever had sex with anyone.

Larkin was clearly good at hiding his true sexual nature — at the very time when he was sharing rooms with Brown, he was writing a series of thinly veiled sexual fantasies and two novels set in an imaginary girls' school, published posthumously in 2002 as *Trouble at Willow Gables and Other Fictions.* Such voyeuristic and prurient tendencies emerge throughout his writings, and may have resulted from his education in a boys' grammar school and an all-male Oxford college: an element of sexual fantasy lies at the heart of *Jill*, his first published novel; the poem 'Sunny Prestatyn' focuses upon the violent and sexually explicit defacing of a poster of a girl in a swimsuit; in 'Wild Oats' the writer is obsessed with the 'bosomy English rose'; and in 'High Windows' the persona imagines the sexual relationship of a young couple he sees walking by. This fascination with sex is reflected in Larkin's predilection for collecting pornography. By the end of his life he had amassed a vast quantity of increasingly explicit material, the discovery of which came as a profound shock to Maeve Brennan.

In the light of this it is not surprising to learn that Larkin held some shockingly unenlightened views on the subject of sex and women, often appearing offensive to the reader. His diaries contain a large number of obscene and sometimes misogynistic observations, a selection of which will suffice to make the point:

> The whole business of sex annoys me. As far as I can see, all women are stupid beings.
>
> Sex is too good to share with anyone else.
>
> Re sexual intercourse: always disappointing and often repulsive, like asking someone else to blow your own nose for you.

Many of these views, pithily expressed and firmly held, form the basis for Larkin's writings about sex and women. Indeed, sex and writing were closely linked in Larkin's mind, as this extract from a letter written to Jim Sutton on 28 December 1942 makes clear:

> ...writing ha[s] got something to do with sex. I don't know what and I don't particularly want to know. It's not surprising because obviously two creative voices would be in alliance. But the vision has a sexual quality lacking in other emotions such as pity...Ovid, for instance, could never write unless he was in love. Many other poets have been or are the same. I should think poetry and sex are very closely connected.

Larkin's views on sex and women are disconcertingly contradictory. He was capable of the greatest cruelty and heartlessness, a trait perhaps most clearly displayed in his deeply ambivalent relationship with Monica Jones. But her testimony shows that he could be a warm and humorous companion. Although at times duplicitous and deceitful, he was also profoundly loyal. A fear of commitment went alongside an inability to be without a relationship or companionship of some kind. All of these features are reflected in his writings.

Larkin and marriage

Throughout his life Larkin was deeply affected by his parents and their marriage. His father and mother had extremely different personalities. Both in their own way had a great influence on him, as he was quick to recognise. In a letter to Jim Sutton of 2 January 1943 he puts it like this:

> I contain both [my mother and my father], and that…is the cause of my inertia, for in me they are incessantly opposed. It intrigues me to know that a thirty year struggle is being continued in me and in my sister too.

The impact of this struggle is most famously summed up in Larkin's poem 'This Be The Verse', from *High Windows,* in which he bluntly observes: 'They fuck you up, your mum and dad./They may not mean to, but they do.'

Marriage, parenthood and the relationship between parents and their children form a recurrent theme in Larkin's work. In *The Whitsun Weddings*, poems such as 'Afternoons', 'Take One Home for the Kiddies', 'Self's the Man', 'Talking in Bed', 'The Whitsun Weddings' and 'Dockery and Son' explore his complex and rigid emotion on the subject. The fact that his determination never to marry or have children was a direct consequence of what he witnessed of his parents' marriage is stated unequivocally in this note from his pocket diary:

> At 1.45 p.m. let me remember that the only married state I know (i.e. that of my parents) is bloody hell. Never must it be forgotten.

It is certain that Larkin never did forget. To the end of his days he fiercely resisted the pressure to marry. Speaking of Larkin's view of marriage, Andrew Motion considers the poem 'Marriages' (from *Collected Poems*), of which he argues:

> [Larkin] mocks partnerships created by 'old need' and 'scarecrows of chivalry'. Admitting that 'rancour' and self-hatred may seem ignoble reasons for demanding solitude, he also says they are justifiable if they manage to hold marriage at bay.
>
> (*Philip Larkin: A Writer's Life*, p. 210)

The nearest Larkin was able to come to the marriage commitment, in spite of his tormenting guilt about the way in which he was treating and using women, was to live with Monica Jones for a brief period at the very end of his life, after she had suffered a debilitating illness.

Jazz

Alan Plater, in the foreword to Larkin's *Jazz: Essays and Reviews 1940–84*, dubs Philip Larkin 'the ultimate jazz freak, alone in his room, tapping his feet and snapping his fingers to the music he loves'. Although for many readers of Larkin's poetry such an image may be difficult to conjure up, the connection between the poet of *The Whitsun Weddings* and jazz was long and profound. From early in life Larkin was a confirmed lover of jazz. While he was growing up in Coventry in the 1930s he became acquainted with radio broadcasts of American jazz and blues, and he frequently attended live performances (getting to know a number of the performers) at the local Hippodrome. He even managed to persuade his parents to buy him a drum kit and a set of tuition records, so keen was he to immerse himself in the world of jazz. Later in life he was to observe: 'I was in essence hooked on jazz even before I heard any...what got me was the rhythm.'

The extent of the influence of jazz on Larkin emerges in the interview 'Poet on the 8.15' (*Guardian*, 20 May 1965), in which he states: 'I can live a week without poetry but not a day without jazz.' The music of 'trad' jazz and blues artists was arguably his greatest love, and an interest he shared with his fellow members of the Movement (see pp. 18–20), and with Kingsley Amis in particular. It was Larkin's passion, but not an uncritical passion. When discussing later and modernist jazz, forms which he found increasingly distasteful, he was often scathing. His comments on the playing of Miles Davis, the trumpeter, serve to illustrate this:

> ...he had several manners: the dead muzzled slow stuff, the sour yelping fast stuff, and the sonorous theatrical arranged stuff, and I disliked them all.

Perhaps this dislike emerged from Larkin's growing sense that jazz was becoming serious, specialist and more overtly 'composed', and that it lacked the easy accessibility of the music he came to love as a young man. In 'Lives of the Poets' (*Guardian*, 24 November 1961), Larkin regrets the extent to which the arts can become stagnant and lifeless, 'generally accepted and subsidised with unenthusiastic reverence'. It was the life and passion, the energy and the emotion of jazz that Larkin wished to preserve.

Despite his eminence as a jazz critic and writer, Larkin always (probably disingenuously) claimed the status of an amateur in the field of music. Describing his connection with jazz, he wrote:

> ...I became a jazz addict at the age of twelve or thirteen...and although far from an expert, have never ceased to be an enthusiast.

In a letter to Steve Race, the music critic and broadcaster, and a confirmed lover of modern jazz, he observed:

> I am not a music lover in any real sense of the word; it is only jazz that won my allegiance.

What perhaps lies behind these statements, apart from the self-effacing intentions of a naturally withdrawn and private man, is the recognition that jazz, while a passion, was never for Larkin an academic exercise. *Torchlight 69* (23 October 1962) recounts a talk given by the poet to a group of students at the University of Hull, where he worked as a librarian, in which he offered the view that:

> ...jazz is to be appreciated not as a musical exercise in technique, but as an emotional experience, one that can exhilarate or sadden.

To borrow Paul Oliver's words, it was the ability of jazz and blues (an apt label in the context of Larkin's famously bleak worldview) 'to meet the present world on its own terms' that Larkin so loved.

What Larkin sought in jazz, then, was emotional experience, not academic and intellectual satisfaction. That is not to say, however, that his responses to jazz were lacking in academic and intellectual depth. Whether he realised it or not, he was both learned and sophisticated in his responses to the music he heard. Primarily, though, he revelled in the rhythms and the passions (maybe even the poetry) excited by jazz. Like poetry, jazz was nothing for Larkin if it could not communicate. Writing to Race in 1968, he put forward the following artistic manifesto, which relates to both jazz and poetry:

> What I don't believe about art is that it should require some special knowledge or special training on the part of its consumers. Art is enjoyment first on the part of the writer, painter or musician, and then, by communication, on the part of the reader and looker and listener.

This principle of pleasure provides a fruitful approach both to Larkin's love of jazz music and to his poetry. It is clear that in Larkin's mind the links between the two forms were deep. Writing of Whitney Balliett, jazz columnist for the *New Yorker*, he observed: 'Balliett...brings jazz journalism to the verge of poetry' (*All What Jazz: A Record Diary 1961–71*, p. 212). This is, of course, also true of Larkin's own jazz journalism. Of equal interest to the student of Larkin's poems, however, is the extent to which he brings poetry to the verge of jazz. Poems such as 'For Sidney Bechet' and 'Reference Back' illustrate the ease with which jazz and poetry intermingle and engage with one another in Larkin's imagination.

The Movement

'The Movement' was a term first employed in 1954 by the literary editor of the *Spectator*, J. D. Scott. He used it to describe a group of English writers (writers from Wales and Scotland are generally excluded), the best known of which are Philip Larkin, Kingsley Amis, Donald Davie, D. J. Enright, John Wain, Elizabeth Jennings and

Robert Conquest. The anti-Romantic, witty, sardonic and rational preoccupations of the writers in the Movement are reflected in the three major anthologies they produced during the 1950s and 1960s. The first of these, *Poets of the 1950s*, was published in 1955 in Japan and was edited by D. J. Enright. The second, and probably the more famous, is *New Lines*, which appeared in 1956, edited by Robert Conquest. A second *New Lines* came out in 1963, drawing in the work of new poets, such as Anthony Thwaite, Ted Hughes, Vernon Scannell and George MacBeth, though by this time the Movement's heyday as a fashionable artistic force had passed.

The Movement was a looser gathering of writers and a less conscious expression of strongly held views about art than the movements of the early twentieth century, such as imagism, surrealism, Fauvism and futurism. It was more a reflection of negative perceptions of what literature had become. This is perhaps best summed up in the words of Conquest's polemical foreword to *New Lines*, where he describes the connections between the poets as 'little more than a negative determination to avoid bad principles'. The anthology particularly targeted the poets of the 1940s, such as Dylan Thomas and George Barker, though never mentioning them by name. The obscure and overly **metaphorical** nature of their verse was the greatest dislike of the Movement authors, and Conquest promotes the cause of 'rational structure and comprehensible language', both of which are readily identified in the works of Philip Larkin, who was nothing if not clear-spoken.

Main works

The main works of the Movement authors other than Larkin are given in the table below. This list is not comprehensive, nor does it include all the authors associated with the Movement, but reading a selection from it will offer an insight into its literary concerns during the 1950s and early 1960s. Most of these authors continued to write well into the 1980s and some into the 1990s. Blake Morrison's book, *The Movement: English Poetry and Fiction of the 1950s* (1980), is an illuminating account of these writers and their work.

Kingsley Amis	
Poetry	*Bright November* (1947), *A Frame of Mind* (1953)
Novels	Thirty in all, starting with *Lucky Jim* (1954), *That Uncertain Feeling* (1955) *I Like It Here* (1958) and *Take a Girl Like You* (1960)
John Braine	
Novels	*Room at the Top* (1957), *Life at the Top* (1962)
Robert Conquest	
Poetry	*Poems* (1955), *Between Mars and Venus* (1962), *Arias from a Love Opera* (1969)
Donald Davie	
Poetry	*Brides of Reason* (1955), *A Winter Talent* (1957)
Criticism	*Purity of Diction in English Verse* (1952)

D. J. Enright	
Poetry	*The Laughing Hyena and Other Poems* (1953), *Bread Rather Than Blossoms* (1956)
Novel	*Insufficient Poppy* (1960)
Criticism	*Man is an Onion: Reviews and Essays* (1972)
Ted Hughes	
Poetry	*The Hawk in the Rain* (1957), *Lupercal* (1960)
Prose and verse	*Wodwo* (1967)
Elizabeth Jennings	
Poetry	*Poems* (1953), *A Way of Looking* (1955), *A Sense of the World* (1958)
George MacBeth	
Poetry	*A Form of Words* (1954), *The Colour of Blood* (1967)
Vernon Scannell	
Poetry	*Graves and Resurrections* (1948), *The Masks of Love* (1960) *Sense of Danger* (1962)
Anthony Thwaite	
Poetry	*Home Truths* (1957), *The Stones of Emptiness: Poems 1963–66* (1967)
John Wain	
Poetry	*Poems 1949–79* (1980)
Novels	*Hurry on Down* (1953), *The Contenders* (1958), *A Travelling Woman* (1959)

The 1960s

The 1960s was a significant decade in British history. The period of austerity which began during the Second World War did not end until the early 1950s. Rationing of food and other items continued until 1954, by which time Larkin had already published two novels, *Jill* and *A Girl in Winter*, and two collections of poetry, *The North Ship* and *XX Poems*. During the late 1950s a number of changes occurred: pop music began to emerge (there is an **allusion** to this in 'Annus Mirabilis', where Larkin identifies the year 1963 by 'the end of the *Chatterley* ban/And the Beatles' first LP'); film became an important influence on young people; televisions and telephones were installed in many British homes (in 'Mr Bleaney', Larkin bemoans the landlady's 'jabbering set'). Together, these led to the revolution of mass media and mass communications.

Post-colonial Britain

Britain was a major imperial power until the Second World War: the British Empire was the largest in the world and spanned the globe. After the war it became clear that the era of empire was over, and the granting of independence to India, Pakistan and Ceylon as early as 1947 was a precursor to the process of wholesale decolonisation which began in the late 1950s (see 'Naturally the Foundation will Bear your Expenses'). This led to two major changes in British society. The first was the mass immigration of non-European people from former colonies, which in time turned Britain into a multiracial society. This was controversial; racism became an issue, and was whipped up by right-wing nationalist politicians, perhaps most famously Enoch Powell. The second change was more subtle: from being a major world power, Britain slowly became a small country in Europe, and many people had difficulty in coming to terms with Britain's loss of importance and influence on the world stage.

Politics and culture

Britain had been a democracy since the nineteenth century, but a combination of factors had led to the right-wing Conservative Party dominating British politics for much of the twentieth century. The left-wing Labour Party came to power in 1964, after 13 years of Conservative rule, and the new government coincided with a period of renewed intellectual and cultural life in the country. It was the era of the Beatles, the most successful pop group ever, of 'Swinging Britain', with its outrageous fashion and personal liberation. The widespread introduction of the contraceptive pill meant that women could have sex without fear of becoming pregnant, and by the end of the 1960s the 'sexual revolution' had swept away centuries of taboos. 'Free love' became popular and male homosexuality became legal for the first time. The 'hippy' movement of the late 1960s seemed to promise an alternative lifestyle that was unconventional, anti-materialist and free-thinking. All these changes broke the stranglehold of conventional morality and class stereotyping that for some had made life in the 1950s and early 1960s stifling. In Larkin's work, however, conservative attitudes continued to hold sway, as if he were a repository of older, outmoded values. This generates a sense of the poet as an outsider, observing a world to which he did not really seem to belong.

Social change

The many social changes of the 1960s particularly affected young people and women. This was the era of pop art, miniskirts, beat music, long hair and hallucinogenic drugs. Young people went to pop festivals and love-ins, and joined the peace movement (which grew out of the Campaign for Nuclear Disarmament).

The feminist movement began to challenge the limitations placed upon women, and there was a feeling among intelligent young women that everything was possible. Grammar schools offered a route to university for lower-middle-class women, who would previously never have considered going, such as Margaret Thatcher (a woman Larkin greatly admired and who subsequently became prime minister). The development of labour-saving domestic appliances, such as washing machines, reduced the burden of domestic tasks. Women increasingly challenged the traditional view that their place was in the home and chose to make careers for themselves.

For Philip Larkin's generation, which had grown up under the deprivations and hardships of the Second World War and the postwar era, the 1960s, with its seemingly limitless freedoms, was a time of ambivalence. While the new freedoms were welcomed by some, they were resented by many and vilified by others. In poems like 'Annus Mirabilis' and 'High Windows' Larkin may celebrate the new-found and overt sexual opportunities that came with increased sexual freedom for women, but in poems such as 'A Study of Reading Habits' and 'Sunny Prestatyn' a more disturbing sense of women as sex objects emerges. The changing face of England and its mores is the subject of a number of Larkin's poems. This theme is particularly evident in Larkin's presentation of the growth of consumer culture, with its attendant emphasis on advertising. He deals with this issue directly in poems such as 'Essential Beauty', 'Here', 'Sunny Prestatyn' and 'Send No Money'. 'MCMXIV' evinces a nostalgia for the innocent old-fashioned advertisements that existed prior to the First World War.

Language

When studying the work of any author it is essential to focus closely on the characteristics of his or her language and to consider its effects in depth. Some of the significant characteristics of Larkin's language are explored below.

Range

Larkin's poetry is notable for the wide range of language it employs, varying from the highly poetic to the obscene. His combination of different **registers** in *The Whitsun Weddings* generates a number of effects. Its realistic synthesis of the moving, the obscene, the elevated, the base, and so on, communicates to a variety of audiences and appeals to a number of emotions. However, it also creates an uneasy sense of linguistic dislocation and might even be said to construct a redefinition of what constitutes 'poetic' diction.

The following table illustrates the variety of tones and registers in *The Whitsun Weddings*.

Precise and incisive description	Qualified or tentative phrasing
'the faint/Archaic smell of dockland' 'The Importance of Elsewhere'	'I don't know.' 'Mr Bleaney'
'Closed like confessionals' 'Ambulances'	'saying so to some/Means nothing; others it leaves Nothing to be said.' 'Nothing to be Said'
'One sees, with a sharp tender shock,/His hand withdrawn, holding her hand.' 'An Arundel Tomb'	'Or I suppose I can.' 'Self's the Man'
'we raced across/Bright knots of rail' 'The Whitsun Weddings'	'Words at once true and kind,/Or not untrue and not unkind.' 'Talking in Bed'
'a terminate and fishy-smelling/Pastoral of ships up streets' 'Here'	'forced to qualify or so I feel,/Or Well, it does seem so:/Someone must know.' 'Ignorance'
	'our almost-instinct almost true' 'An Arundel Tomb'

Colloquial, unpoetic language	Poetic diction and description
'Were itching to have a bash' 'Send No Money' 'her face/Was snaggle-toothed and boss-eyed' 'Sunny Prestatyn' 'Get stewed' 'A Study of Reading Habits' 'he egged her on' 'Mr Bleaney' 'Oh, play that thing!' 'For Sidney Bechet' 'the kiddies' clobber' 'Self's the Man'	'their cut-off shout/Leaving me desperate to pick out/Your hands, tiny in all that air, applauding.' 'Broadcast' 'Here is unfenced existence:/Facing the sun, untalkative, out of reach.' 'Here' 'there swelled/A sense of falling, like an arrow-shower/Sent out of sight, somewhere becoming rain.' 'The Whitsun Weddings' 'The glare of that much-mentioned brilliance, love,/Broke out, to show/Its bright incipience sailing above' 'Love Songs in Age'
Coarse and obscene language	**Sharp, harsh diction**
'Books are a load of crap.' 'A Study of Reading Habits' 'A tuberous cock and balls' 'Sunny Prestatyn' 'Sod all.' 'Send No Money'	'It used to make me throw up,/These mawkish nursery games' 'Naturally the Foundation will Bear your Expenses' 'The women I clubbed with sex!' 'A Study of Reading Habits'

Hyphenated words

Larkin uses hyphenated words throughout *The Whitsun Weddings* to create precise meanings through word combinations:

- In 'Love Songs in Age', the woman's memory 'ushered in/Word after sprawling hyphenated word' — this suggests the unstoppable and continual flow of images from the past.
- The 'Sunday-full and organ-frowned-on spaces' of 'Broadcast' creates the image of seriousness, even severity, that surrounds the formal concert, and suggests the crammed in members of the audience.
- In 'Toads Revisited', 'My shall-I-keep-the-call-in-Sir' re-creates the hurried and familiar speech of the secretary and suggests office routine.
- In 'Water', 'any-angled light' is an **image** of illumination or enlightenment from a variety of directions and sources, which fits in with the poem's idea of creating a community of faith that turns diversity into unity.
- The build-up of hyphenated words in 'Small-statured cross-faced tribes/And cobble-close families' ('Nothing to be Said') simultaneously establishes points of contrast and of comparison between peoples. The image of 'cobble-close families', with its suggestion of narrow streets, is especially evocative of intimacy forged through proximity in humble circumstances.
- In 'The Whitsun Weddings' there is 'A sense of falling, like an arrow-shower' — the combination of the natural and the deadly captures the ambivalent attitude towards marriage in this poem.

Negative language

Throughout *The Whitsun Weddings* there are numerous words beginning with the prefixes 'dis-', 'im-', 'ir-', 'non-' and 'un-' or ending with the suffix '-less' to indicate negativity. The accumulation of these negative forms emphasises the extent to which Larkin's verse entails negative definition: things are frequently described by what they are not rather than by what they are. This leaves a sense of inadequacy and unfulfilment, the feeling that there is something lacking. The repeated use of negatives throughout *The Whitsun Weddings* ('no', 'not', 'none', 'never', 'nothing', 'nobody', 'nowhere', 'no one' etc.) also creates a sense of definition through absence. The accretion of such vocabulary contributes to the pervading sense of negativity that underlies Larkin's famously bleak worldview. The table below categorises these negative forms.

dis-	displaced, dismantled, disproved
im-	immeasurable, imprecisions
ir-	irresolutely
non-	nondescript
un-	unknown, unlucky, unfocused, unfair, untransferable, unripe, undated, unarmorial, untruth, unnoticed, unfenced, untalkative, unfailing, unchangeably, unreally, uneven, unrest, undiminished, untrue, unkind, unearthly, unreal, unbitten, unreachable, unworkable, unwelcome, unlike, unhindered, unsatisfactory
-less	restless, shamelessly, natureless, sunless, soundless, endless, helpless

Themes

The key themes of *The Whitsun Weddings* are listed below, with details of poems in which each appears and comments on how it is treated.

Women and marriage

Larkin displays a jaded view of women and marriage throughout *The Whitsun Weddings*. Only at the end of his life was Larkin able to commit himself to living with his long-term partner, Monica Jones, though the moral and emotional pressure to marry and 'make an honest woman' of both her and Maeve Brennan, another of his long-term girlfriends, was something that continually tormented him.

This refusal to marry was a reaction to his parents' marriage, which he saw as profoundly unhappy and destructive (see p. 16). Speaking of his father, Larkin observed:

> It would be somewhat absurd of me to regret his marriage, but I could never see why he needed a wife. He liked his own company best and gloried in his ability to look after himself, and his clumsiness in human relations must have made him an unsatisfactory husband, which in turn must have put a certain strain on him.

> Certainly the marriage left me with two convictions: that human beings should not live together, and that children should be taken from their parents at an early age.
>
> (The Philip Larkin Archive, Brynmor Jones Library, Notebook 5)

The following poems all offer interesting insights into Larkin's views on women and marriage:

'Love Songs in Age'

The tenderness of this portrait of a disappointed and now lonely widow is at odds with the representation of women elsewhere in the collection. Love and marriage are initially held up as an ideal — the woman keeps her songs as sentimental mementos. Remembering, however, paints a different and painful picture. She realises that love does not and never did 'solve, and satisfy,/And set unchangeably in order'.

'Broadcast'

This poem was written for and about Maeve Brennan, and offers a yearning portrait of a woman as the object of desire. Like 'Love Songs in Age', its tenderness marks it out from the rest of the collection. The narrator's efforts to picture his beloved at the concert and to hear her applause suggest deep affection. However, words such as 'dark', 'lose' and 'desperate' hint at the difficulty of forging a connection with a loved one.

'Faith Healing'

In this poem women are portrayed as passive dupes of the charlatan faith healer (the word 'sheepishly' connotes both biddableness and embarrassment or shame). Although they display a range of conflicting feelings, the overwhelming emotion suffered by all of them is lack of love.

'For Sidney Bechet'

The women here are prostitutes: 'Sporting-house girls like circus tigers (priced//Far above rubies)'. The word 'tigers' implies that they are both beautiful and dangerous, but they are 'circus tigers', subject to the will of their handler.

'Self's the Man'

This poem conveys a cynical and sexist view of women as possessions ('He married a woman to stop her getting away'); as burdens and drains ('the money he gets for wasting his life on work/She takes as her perk'); and as demanding nags ('when he finishes supper/Planning to have a read at the evening paper/It's *Put a screw in this wall*'). It isn't any less bleak in its presentation of marriage; getting married is initially presented as more generous than remaining single ('Arnold is less selfish than I'), but eventually marriage is judged to come from selfish desires too: Arnold is 'out for his own ends', as is his wife, looking for 'her perk'. In this regard neither sex emerges positively.

'MCMXIV'

Marriages in this poem are doomed to come to an end, but because of the First World War, not for personal reasons. However, the lines 'thousands of marriages/ Lasting a little while longer' imply that it is because the men are going off to war, 'leaving the gardens tidy', that the marriages will last for a while more — absence makes the heart grow fonder.

'Talking in Bed'

Intimate conversation in bed starts as 'An emblem of two people being honest'. However, it grows harder to balance honesty with kindness: 'It becomes still more difficult to find/Words at once true and kind,/Or not untrue and not unkind.' Talking (the measure of this relationship) falls away as 'more and more time passes silently', while the weather conditions suggest growing turmoil and discomfort.

'A Study of Reading Habits'

While not exclusively about women, this poem nevertheless presents some disturbing views. It describes the brutal sexual fantasies of the narrator as a young man ('The women I clubbed with sex!/I broke them up like meringues') and the **stereotypical** unreliability of male characters in books: 'the dude/Who lets the girl down before/The hero arrives'.

'Sunny Prestatyn'

The description of the poster initially seems a straightforward depiction of a typical seaside advert, but as the poem progresses the tone becomes more sexually voyeuristic: the background seems to 'expand from her thighs and/Spread breast-lifting arms'. Violence enters at stanza 2 with the disturbing implications of 'slapped up' and anticipates the grotesque desecration of her body — 'Huge tits and a fissured crotch' — while the description of her as 'set...fairly astride/A tuberous cock and balls' is like an act of rape. The woman is at first presented as a sex object, then as a victim of abuse and assault; the moustache is an aggressive desexualisation or cancellation of her womanliness.

'Wild Oats'

In this poem, physical attraction does not lead to sexual fulfilment. The **persona** presents two types of women: a sexually attractive one ('A bosomy English rose') and a plainer but more approachable one ('her friend in specs I could talk to'). Neither of them is named, and their anonymity reduces them to objects of the male gaze. The persona's seven-year-long relationship with the second woman may have involved extra-marital sex ('met/At numerous cathedral cities/Unknown to the clergy'), but ultimately resulted in returned gifts and recriminations about his inability to love. The phrase 'wild oats', with its connotations of illicit sexual activity and wild living, is also significant.

'Afternoons'

Married life is presented as uniform and orderly — neat assemblies of mothers and rows of fathers — and as lacking spontaneity and originality. The wedding album has no special place, but is simply 'lying/Near the television'. By ending the line with the word 'lying', Larkin emphasises its double meaning, hinting at the false picture of marriage constructed by the album. The past (symbolised by the couples' 'courting-places') is being erased. The couples are succeeded by much younger lovers and are becoming marginalised within their own lives by the march of time and the demands of their children.

Children

In 'This Be The Verse', Larkin observes that parents 'fuck you up', but also how they 'were fucked up in their turn', a process that will never end, as 'Man hands on misery to man'. He offers a solution: 'Get out as early as you can,/And don't have any kids yourself.' His dislike of children is evident in the following poems in *The Whitsun Weddings*:

'Afternoons'

Children appear as a powerful and demanding force in this poem. Parents set their children free and are then **ironically** imprisoned by them. The parents' freedom to do as they wish is clearly curtailed by their children, who act as one of the factors marginalising the adults within their own lives. This emphasises the distance, even the division, Larkin perceives between parents and their children.

'Self's the Man'

Larkin's dislike of what children represent is apparent here. They are significant factors, along with marriage, in limiting the free existence of the persona's friend, Arnold. Children are a means of perpetuating misery down the generations.

'Take One Home for the Kiddies'

This poem suggests Larkin's feeling that children are a species apart and unapproachable. It also suggests the ease with which children become bored, rapidly moving from one preoccupation to the next. The title of the poem indicates how children are used as a lever in marketing, promoting consumerism.

'Dockery and Son'

The philosophical and personal issues the poem addresses profoundly question the parent/child relationship and the reasons why people enter into it. This indicates Larkin's dislike of the notion of having children and his lack of comprehension about why people would willingly choose to procreate.

Death

Death is a recurrent theme not only in *The Whitsun Weddings* but throughout Larkin's work. In 'The Old Fools' (*High Windows*), he refers to death as 'The peak that stays in view wherever we go': we are perpetually aware of it. For Larkin, death is an integral part of the experience of living.

In 'Nothing to be Said', death is seen as the inevitable end of all existence, a leveller of humanity regardless of ethnicity, background or occupation. 'Take One Home for the Kiddies' offers a dark view of death as the end to lives that were cheap and disposable. The cynical answer to the question posed in 'Days' —'Where can we live but days?' — appears to be death, as it 'Brings the priest and the doctor/In their long coats/Running over the fields'.

In 'Ignorance', life and experience do not lead to wisdom, but only to deeper uncertainty. Even death brings no clarification: we 'spend all our life on imprecisions,/That when we start to die/Have no idea why.' 'MCMXIV' ushers in the First World War with all its death and destruction, but also captures the death of an era and the death of innocence.

More positively, 'An Arundel Tomb' reflects upon what is left of us after we die. The monument to the couple creates a possibly untruthful impression of how they lived, but conveys the positive message that 'What will survive of us is love'.

For a full discussion on death in 'Dockery and Son', see pp. 57–60.

Isolation

Larkin generally presents isolation in a favourable light. In 'The Importance of Elsewhere', he explores the benefits associated with being a stranger or an outsider. He identifies the indulgence that is afforded to people unfamiliar with local ways, allowances which would not be made for somebody born and bred locally: strangeness and foreignness 'underwrites my existence'. The persona of the poem finds comfort in the newness and separation that comes with the new environment. This is emphasised when he observes how 'strangeness made sense' and 'difference made me welcome'. In the end he finds meaning and new dimensions of himself in the new place, concluding that in his new home he is 'separate, not unworkable'.

Isolation plays a similar role in 'Here'. Far from separating the persona from existence, it brings him into a new and deeper contact with himself. Hull, though apart from the frenetic activity of the motorway, is still a place of busyness and activity, isolated but not a place of freedom. It is when the narrator goes onto the Holderness peninsula, with its 'Isolate villages' and the 'removed lives' of their inhabitants, that he finds himself in true and meaningful isolation. The experience does not leave him lonely, but almost spiritually elevated and engaged. His final observation that 'Loneliness clarifies' expresses the liberation he senses.

'The Whitsun Weddings' begins in the pleasant and indulgent isolation of the 'three-quarters-empty train'. Loneliness here is a positive pleasure for the narrator, who luxuriates in its warmth, comfort and opportunity to sleep. As the train moves southwards, picking up its plethora of married couples, isolation in its purest sense disappears as the carriages become crowded. The narrator, however, by virtue of his singleness, remains alone, and consciously voyeuristic of the young couples surrounding him. The journey is a shared experience, but one in which he is very much an observer. As in 'Here', the reader is left with a sense of spiritual enlightenment, as the poem prefigures the isolation of the married state that will eventually face the newlyweds.

'Self's the Man' compares the states of marriage and singleness and weighs the position of the individual in each. Although he hasn't a wife or 'nippers', the single man is in many ways no more isolated than the married man, who has to give up so much of his individuality to make his marriage work. While singleness can be seen as isolating in its lack of companionship, marriage is isolating for Arnold, whose life is presented as a continual round of constraints. Unlike the poems discussed above, 'Self's the Man' does not give isolation a positive slant.

Disillusionment and futility

At the heart of 'Ignorance' is a sense that a lack of knowledge and understanding makes for a futile existence. Larkin goes so far as to question the usefulness of knowledge at all: 'it is strange,//Even to wear such knowledge'. The pursuit of 'imprecisions', and the conflict between bodily and intellectual demands, lead to the confusion the poem ends on. In 'Send No Money', the mock-oracle Time gives a message of futile passivity: '*Sit here, and watch the hail/Of occurrence clobber life out/To a shape no one sees*'. Following this depressing advice leads only to further disillusionment; in the final stanza, the older man, looking back on his wasted youth, observes that it has brought him 'Sod all'.

The questions in stanza 1 of 'Days' suggest the pointlessness of existence. Life is reduced to a dull cycle of repetition ('they wake us/Time and time over'), and the only meaning attributable to life is its ending. Similarly, in 'Nothing to be Said', the conclusion of the opening stanza, 'Life is slow dying', suggests life's painful futility. The poem concludes that the pointlessness of life either 'Means nothing' or 'leaves/Nothing to be Said' — both outcomes are empty.

Mr Bleaney and his successor in the rented rooms lead limited and humdrum lives. The futility and impoverishment of their existence is summed up in the final observation that Mr Bleaney has 'no more to show/Than one hired box' — a reference to the rented room, but also an allusion to the coffin in which Mr Bleaney will end up. The woman in 'Love Songs in Age' is forced to recognise that her romantic idealisation of love is just an illusion. She painfully comes to realise that its 'much-mentioned brilliance' is ultimately unsatisfying.

In 'Dockery and Son', disillusionment strikes after the funeral, when the traveller experiences 'numbness' at realising 'how much had gone of life'. The change at Sheffield is not only a change of trains; it is also a change in his view of life. His 'Innate assumptions' about life and its meaning are challenged, leading to the conclusion that 'Life is first boredom, then fear', a futile transition on the way to death, 'the only end of age'. A change also occurs to the onlookers in 'Ambulances' who see the patients on the stretchers. They are suddenly made aware of 'the solving emptiness/That lies just under all we do...So permanent and blank and true'. The episode 'dulls to distance all we are' — a reminder of death that makes existence seem futile.

Truth

In 'Send No Money', the young man asks the portentous figure of Time for enlightenment: '*Tell me the truth,* I said,/*Teach me the way things go.*' Time's advice eventually proves worthless and the older man knows he has wasted his youth in 'Tracing the trite untransferable/Truss-advertisement, truth'.

Truth is suspect elsewhere in the collection. The advertisements in 'Essential Beauty' are the embodiment of untruthful glitz. Their manufactured perfection determines the consumer's view of 'how life should be', but there is no resemblance between this and the vomiting, poverty, dirtiness and cancer in stanza 2, which are the true realities of life. In 'Dockery and Son', hearing about Dockery Junior causes the nameless friend to recognise that he did not know the truth about his old college friend, Dockery Senior. This prompts him to re-evaluate his existence and to question his own true nature. The 'Innate assumptions' of our lives, the 'truths' we cling on to and build our lives around, become the blinding 'sand-clouds, thick and close' that prevent our seeing the truth of life.

Similarly seeking to understand his unsatisfactory life, the narrator of 'Reference Back' states: 'Truly, though our element is time,/We are not suited to the long perspectives'. As proof of this, he goes on to observe how the enlightenment that comes with the reference back painfully forces us to recognise the truth of how we have changed and what we have lost in doing so. In 'Talking in Bed', it grows harder as time passes for this couple to be truthful about their feelings for each other without being cruel: 'It becomes still more difficult to find/Words at once true and kind,/Or not untrue and not unkind.'

You should refer also to the discussion of 'An Arundel Tomb' on pp. 60–65.

Time

Larkin had a particular fascination with time. He was always alert to the social changes he saw going on around him, and in many ways felt that he belonged neither to the old nor to the new. He was profoundly aware of the imperatives of time, both linear (the movement from birth to death) and cyclical (repetition and cycles).

Specific times of day and references to the passage of time are found in 'Ambulances' ('Loud noons of cities'); 'Wild Oats' ('About twenty years ago'); 'Mr Bleaney' (his routine is an attempt to fill time); 'Faith Healing' ('Each dwells some twenty seconds'); 'Home is so Sad' (a forlorn stasis is evoked in which time seems to stand still); 'Sunny Prestatyn' ('one day in March'); 'The Whitsun Weddings' ('One-twenty on the sunlit Saturday'; 'their lives would all contain this hour'); 'Dockery and Son' ('Anyone up today must have been born/in '43'); 'MCMXIV' (the year the First World War started).

Elsewhere, time is used to show the monotony of existence. 'Nothing to be Said' is about the march of time and the insignificance of life. There are two references to 'slow dying', and units of time ('day' and 'Hours') are described as moving 'slowly', wasted on pointless and meaningless activities. The title of 'Days' (like 'Afternoons') draws attention to time; the poem focuses on the repetition of daily life: 'Days are where we live./They come, they wake us/Time and time over.' This repetition is evident in 'Toads Revisited', in which time serves as a measure of the strangely comforting but ultimately pointless round of working life: 'Hearing the hours chime,//Watching the bread delivered'.

Time also reveals the pointlessness of life in 'Reference Back', which begins with the narrator 'Wasting my time at home'; a recording of 'Oliver's *Riverside Blues*' foreshortens time, taking the narrator back to 'The year after I was born', as well as creating a 'sudden bridge' between him and his elderly parent. The 'long perspectives' bring a realisation of the shortness of life and how little it amounts to. Time appears in 'Send No Money' as a mock-oracle who advises the narrator to study life for its hidden meaning; the narrator follows this advice but comes to the conclusion that there is no meaning and he has wasted his time. However, in 'Water', time is transcended, as the poet envisages 'A glass of water/Where any-angled light/Would congregate endlessly'.

See also the discussion of 'An Arundel Tomb' (pp. 60–65).

Music

Larkin's passion for 'trad' jazz and blues is unmistakably reflected in *The Whitsun Weddings*. In some poems music is a powerful and potentially life-giving (although never an unambiguous) force, but it often serves only to point up the inadequacy of other experiences and emotions by comparison.

'For Sidney Bechet'

Sidney Bechet (1897–1959) was an influential New Orleans saxophonist. The opening lines of the poem encapsulate the excitement and emotion aroused by the music: 'That note you hold, narrowing and rising, shakes/Like New Orleans reflected on the water'. New Orleans was an important jazz centre, and Larkin transports the reader to the dusky, smoky heat of a New Orleans jazz bar, where 'scholars *manqués*' sit absorbed in their passion for music.

The music is a power of creation within the poet's and the audience's imagination: 'Building for some a legendary Quarter/Of balconies, flower-baskets and quadrilles'. It is an overwhelming, almost sexual force, falling on the narrator 'as they say love should,/Like an enormous yes', a strongly affirmative simile. The last line of the poem can be read in two ways, depending on how the verb 'scattering' is understood. If it is taken to mean 'dispelling', the line suggests that the listeners turn to the music for relief from the 'long-haired grief and scored pity' of other types of music. This contrasts the free and improvisatory nature of jazz with the rigid nature of other types of music. If, however, we take 'scattering' to mean 'distributing' (relating to the imagery of seeds employed throughout the collection), then the line may refer to the musical roots of jazz in Negro spiritual and blues, music notable for its use of 'grief' and 'pity'.

'Love Songs in Age'

The emotions associated with music are ambivalent here. Music is related to memories which appear to be good ('She kept her songs, they took so little space,/The covers pleased her') but ultimately prove a source of sadness and disillusionment. Sun-bleached and water-stained, damaged by the children and then mended, the musical scores evoke memories of homely domesticity, but they also arouse nostalgia for lost youth and unfulfilled promise. Like 'For Sidney Bechet', 'Love Songs in Age' leaves the reader with a sense of the blues. In this case it is more profound, because this poem lacks the affirmation that is present in 'For Sidney Bechet'.

'Reference Back'

A similar sense of retrospective loss (or the blues) to that in 'Love Songs in Age' is found in 'Reference Back'. In this poem a jazz record recalls the narrator's own past and the time when the recording was made. It provides a temporary connection (a 'sudden bridge') between the narrator and his elderly parent.

Within the 'unsatisfactory' home in which the poem is set, music offers escape from humdrum reality. The magical effect of 'The flock of notes those antique Negroes blew/Out of Chicago air into/A huge remembering pre-electric horn', traversing the decades like the beating wings of birds, poignantly heightens the persona's present sense of inadequacy and loss. The freedom of the music and the energy of the musicians contrast with the boredom he feels during his visit home, which he spends 'idly,/Wasting my time'.

'Broadcast'

This poem concerns a radio broadcast of orchestral music. The 'Giant whispering and coughing from/Vast Sunday-full and organ-frowned-on spaces' conjures up a crowded and echoing cathedral. In 'Lives of the Poets' (*Guardian*, 24 November 1961), Larkin refers to the 'subsidised and unenthusiastic reverence' with which 'the established arts' are accepted. This is the atmosphere he creates here, with the humorous invocation of the 'scuttle on the drum,/"The Queen", and huge resettling', and the audience sitting 'Beautiful and devout before/Cascades of monumental slithering'. The narrator is not listening to the concert out of interest in the music but because his girlfriend or wife is in the audience. He imagines her sitting in familiar clothes and tries to make out the sound of her 'tiny' hands amid all the clapping.

Imagery

Movement and distance

The concept of the journey and its metaphorical connection to the journey of life is significant throughout *The Whitsun Weddings.*

- 'Here' — this poem traces the persona's physical and spiritual movement. It begins with the idea of travel — 'traffic all night north' — but the persona is set apart from the majority of these travellers as he is 'Swerving east'. The pace of the journey slows as he reaches Hull and then goes beyond to the Holderness, where a further change in the pace of the poem occurs. The poem ends with a yearning to move 'beyond', past the confines of the land. This signifies the persona's spiritual desire to move beyond the physical limitations of this world into the 'luminously-peopled air' and the endlessness he finds in the isolation of the coast.
- 'The Whitsun Weddings' — reversing the direction of 'Here', this poem traces a journey south, from Hull to London. The journey becomes a symbol for life and the futures of the newlywed couples who join the train on its way to the capital, the hub of all experience. The pace of the poem also reverses the dynamics of 'Here': while 'Here' slows as it moves towards its transcendent conclusion, 'The Whitsun Weddings' speeds up, like an unstoppable 'arrow-shower' towards the final destination with its unknown endings. Like 'Here' and 'Dockery and Son', the notion of the physical journey is closely allied to a spiritual journey and awakening.
- 'Dockery and Son' — as in 'Here' and 'The Whitsun Weddings', physical and spiritual movement combine in this poem. The train journey to Sheffield is the crux of the persona's development. As he envisages the train lines joining and parting he becomes aware of his own development since leaving Oxford and sees how he has become distanced from his fellow students over time, specifically over the issue of children, the central concern of the poem.
- 'Reference Back' — in this poem Larkin explores the emotional distance between a mother and her son. This is a key issue in 'Self's the Man', where the difference between friends is explored, and 'Talking in Bed' and 'Afternoons', where marriage comes under scrutiny.

- 'An Arundel Tomb' — this poem deals with the movement of time and its impact on our understanding of truth. The distance between the 'pre-baroque' and our own 'unarmorial age' is in one sense vast, but is bridged (as time is in 'Reference Back' through Oliver's *Riverside Blues*) by a continuous line of people visiting the tomb. Larkin evokes the couple's 'supine stationary voyage': although physically they have not moved, time has wrought a change in them and our perceptions of what they are.

Seeds

Seeds occur on many occasions throughout *The Whitsun Weddings*. They suggest ongoing life and the attempt to propagate or reproduce (sperm is sometimes called seed). The image frequently relates to making choices and the implications of those choices for the future. Significant examples occur in the following poems:

- 'Here' — Hull's 'grain-scattered streets' provide a contrast to the stark modernity of the clustering spires and cranes, suggesting the ongoing existence of an older and perhaps more frutiful way of life. The rusticity of the image helps provide a bridge from the city to its agricultural surrounds.
- 'The Whitsun Weddings' — the image of the 'arrow-shower' suggests the dissemination of seed, an image connected to the theme of marriage.
- 'Wild Oats' — the notion of sowing seed is present in the title of this poem, which has clear sexual overtones appropriate to the poem's content.
- 'As Bad as a Mile' — the seeds in the apple core are symbolic of potential, both for success and for failure, and aiming at a basket suggests making choices. The 'apple unbitten' could refer to the story of Adam and Eve and the choice they made.
- 'Dockery and Son' — in this poem Larkin questions why humans feel the need to spread their seed. He debates whether seed spreading leads to an increase or a dilution of the self.
- 'Afternoons' — this is another poem dealing with the unsatisfactory relations between parents and their children (their seed). The image of the unripe acorns implies fruitlessness and a lack of completion.
- 'Ignorance' — the 'punctual spread of seed' is one of the characteristics of ignorance, seeming to represent thoughtlessness and lack of awareness of potential consequences.
- Children are the (usually undesirable) result of spreading seed in *The Whitsun Weddings*, e.g. 'Self's the Man', 'Take One Home for the Kiddies', 'First Sight', 'Afternoons' and 'Dockery and Son'.

Lines

Lines in *The Whitsun Weddings* represent direction and purposefulness (whether this is well or badly directed); restraint and the impossibility of change; queues and orderliness; and the notion of the family line. Key examples occur in the following poems:

- 'Here' — Larkin contrasts the curving lines of 'Swerving east' with the direct lines of the M1 heading north and 'The dead straight miles' of Hull's tram network. The curve east is towards the Holderness and 'unfenced existence'; 'dead straight' illustrates the orderliness of the city, but may also suggest that urban life is in some way dead.
- 'Faith Healing' — the line of expectant women waiting to see the faith healer seems to represent unthinking devotion and hope (compare the queues of 'MCMXIV').
- 'The Whitsun Weddings' — the railway lines converge on London, suggesting inescapable direction. The line of the horizon is a significant image in the opening stanza of the poem ('Where sky and Lincolnshire and water meet'), suggesting a future that remains out of reach. The image of the horizon occurs again in 'Talking in Bed', where it has threatening overtones. The focus on marriage and the movement from one generation to the next brings out the importance of the family line, a key issue in 'Dockery and Son'.
- 'MCMXIV' — this poem is dominated by two types of line: the 'long uneven lines' of men queuing to enlist for war and the image of the trenches ('Shadowing Domesday lines').
- Lines of streets are important in both 'Ambulances' and 'The Large Cool Store'. In the latter poem lines of various kinds are important; the streets of 'low terraced houses' are the homes of factory workers who labour on the production lines to produce new lines of clothing for the stores.
- 'Dockery and Son' — this is another poem in which railway lines are significant, representing journeys and the potential different directions life can take. The title of the poem implies the 'business' of continuing the family line.
- 'An Arundel Tomb' — as in 'Faith Healing' and 'MCMXIV', the image of a line of people is important in this poem. It connects the period of the 'pre-baroque' with the 'unarmorial' present.

Single men

Unmarried throughout his life, Larkin remained fascinated with the image of the single man, including it regularly in *The Whitsun Weddings* in a number of roles:

- a figure of selfish detachment, trying to create meaning for himself ('Mr Bleaney')
- a seeker of pleasure ('For Sidney Bechet')
- a voyeur ('Sunny Prestatyn')
- violent and crude ('Sunny Prestatyn')
- seeking to justify his decision not to enter a relationship ('Self's the Man')
- confused and seeking self-definition ('Dockery and Son')

Clothing

The clothes described in 'Faith Healing' suggest the characteristics of the healer, who is coldly and calculatingly smart in his 'rimless glasses, silver hair,/Dark suit, white collar', and of the vulnerable women who have come for healing in their 'flowered frocks'.

In 'For Sidney Bechet', the 'old plaids' of stanza 4 are an essential feature of the men who wear them — a well-worn, comfortable (probably frayed) definition of what the men themselves are. Similarly, in 'Broadcast' clothes serve to define. The 'gloves unnoticed on the floor' and the 'new, slightly-outmoded shoes' are central aspects of the beloved's personality, attractive to the lover listening to the radio and alive in his imagination.

In 'The Whitsun Weddings', Larkin repeatedly draws the reader's attention to the wedding outfits worn by the various parties on the station platforms. They become a vibrant (often tasteless) expression of love and marriage and the collective celebration of it. Clothes (or the lack of them) in 'Sunny Prestatyn' are used to titillate. The 'tautened white satin' the girl wears serves only to draw attention to 'her thighs and/Spread breast-lifting arms'. 'The Large Cool Store', 'Here' and 'Essential Beauty' all use clothes to symbolise the deceptive and hollow glitz of consumerism, whereas in 'Ignorance' Larkin employs the language of dress to describe knowledge, as if it is only a garment to be put on or cast aside: 'it is strange,//Even to wear such knowledge'.

Religion

In 'Faith Healing', Larkin adopts a typically cynical stance towards the apparently predatory faith healer, who plays upon the hopes and fears of his female followers. Religion is clearly an important issue in 'The Whitsun Weddings', which focuses on marriage. The wedding ceremony itself is not scrutinised, but Larkin's ambivalence towards marriage ('a happy funeral') is clear. '[R]eligious wounding' refers to the rupturing of the hymen (Hymen was the Greek and Roman god of marriage), which is sanctioned by the Church. The Whitsun (meaning 'White Sunday') weekend is a popular time for weddings as it often coincides with the first good weather of the year. Although 'An Arundel Tomb' is set in a church and draws on the idea of religious ceremony, the church building and the tomb primarily convey a strong sense of history and the passage of time.

In 'Water', Larkin imagines a religion of his own invention. His focus on the symbolic significance of water bears similarities to the importance of water in Christianity, and some of the vocabulary in the poem is from the Christian faith (e.g. 'church', 'liturgy', 'devout', 'congregate'). However, Larkin's religion is intended to be non-denominational and inclusive. In 'Essential Beauty', 'Here' and 'The Large Cool Store', consumerism appears to be almost an alternative religion.

Railways

Railways are lines coming from a hub, an important pattern of imagery in Larkin's verse. Railway imagery appears to striking effect in *Jill*, Larkin's first novel, an extract of which is reproduced on pp. 72–73. It is important in 'The Whitsun Weddings' (see pp. 52–57) and 'Dockery and Son' (see pp. 57–60).

In 'Here', railways evoke isolation, as the train veers away from the busy road towards Hull, 'swerving to solitude', and physical exertion: 'now and then a harsh-named halt, that shields/Workmen at dawn'. By contrast to the liberating train, the poem refers to the 'stealing flat-faced trolleys' (trams) in the city, which do not travel on the satisfying curve of the railway tracks but 'down/The dead straight miles'.

Consumerism

In 'Essential Beauty', Larkin deconstructs the consumer culture, pointing out its falsity, deception and hollowness. The perfect world conjured up by the advertisers, with its golden butter, fabulous weather, perfect families, contented animals and cosy homes, is starkly in contrast to 'our live imperfect eyes', 'the boy puking his heart out in the Gents', the pensioner over-charged for a cup of tea and the smoker dying of cancer. In 'The Large Cool Store', Larkin suggests the hollowness and meaninglessness of the vast array of clothes in the shop. Far from offering definition and personality, these clothes are an expression of 'unreal wishes', 'synthetic, new/And natureless'. One of the main features of Arnold's wife in 'Self's the Man' is her focus on 'the kiddies' clobber and the drier/And the electric fire'. The family's life is represented as revolving around consumption.

The titles of 'Take One Home for the Kiddies' and 'Send No Money' resemble sales slogans. The former tempts the parents to buy the ill-fated pets, which are seen as little more than disposable goods by the children, whereas the latter promises something for nothing. The advertisement featuring the girl in 'Sunny Prestatyn' is an example of 'sex-sell'. The glamorous image is soon defaced, torn and replaced, suggesting the temporary and disposable nature of the consumer culture. By contrast, the old-fashioned 'tin advertisements' that appear in 'MCMXIV' seem more honest than the glitzy ones that appear in 'Essential Beauty' and 'Sunny Prestatyn'. They represent an innocence that has now been corrupted.

See also the discussion of 'Here' (pp. 47–49).

Water

Water is associated with pain in 'Faith Healing', in which the women cry 'deep hoarse tears' and 'their eyes squeeze grief'. In stanza 3, 'thawing, the rigid landscape weeps'. This is comparable to the appearance of water in 'The Whitsun Weddings', which ends with a foreboding image of rain. By contrast, in 'Water' Larkin draws on its religious symbolism, such as baptism, ritual cleansing, the spiritual journey and refreshment.

Fish docks appear on a number of occasions, creating a particular atmosphere. In 'Here', there is 'a terminate and fishy-smelling/Pastoral of ships up streets'; in 'The Importance of Elsewhere', Larkin invokes 'the faint/Archaic smell of dockland'; and in 'The Whitsun Weddings', the traveller's journey begins on the train where he 'smelt the fish-dock'.

The water on the base of a vase in the opening stanza of 'Love Songs in Age' leaves its mark on the covers, adding to the weight of memory in the poem.

Clouds

Gathering clouds mark an ominous change in the weather, and Larkin uses them to convey bleakness, a threatening future or some other difficulty. The bleating of the lambs in 'First Sight' 'clouds the air' — this combines a physical description of steaming breath in cold spring air with an allusion to the unclear future of innocent new lambs in a harsh environment. It may also be worth noting that sheep resemble clouds. In 'Toads Revisited', Larkin refers to 'The sun by clouds covered': the slightly awkward inversion of this phrase adds to the awkwardness of the people he describes. Clouds appear twice in 'Dockery and Son'; as the narrator leaves Oxford, 'Canal and clouds and colleges subside', creating an image of loss; later, assumptions and values 'rear/Like sand-clouds, thick and close', which suggests oppressive pressure. In 'Mr Bleaney', 'the frigid wind/Tousling the clouds' gives an insight into his bleak and pitiful life. It suggests coldness ('frigid') and lack of care ('Tousling'). Larkin uses clouds in 'Talking in Bed' to convey the troubled state of the relationship the poem dissects: 'the wind's incomplete unrest/Builds and disperses clouds about the sky'. However, clouds are used differently in 'Here'; the 'piled gold clouds' as the traveller approaches Hull are a positive image, not blocking the sun as they do in 'Toads Revisited', but beautified by it.

Nature and plants

Larkin uses nature and plant imagery throughout the collection with various effects:

- 'First Sight' — Larkin does not idealise nature and the lot of the newborn lambs.
- 'Home is so Sad' — the house is represented as a plant, withering in the absence of its inhabitants.
- The natural world plays a significant role in the descriptive passages of 'Here' and 'The Whitsun Weddings'. In both poems it creates a sense of vitality and abundance.
- Flowers are significant images in 'For Sidney Bechet', 'Love Songs in Age', 'Mr Bleaney', 'Toads Revisited' and 'Faith Healing'. Their fragile beauty suggests a world of assaulted and fractured innocence.

- 'Wild Oats' — one of the two girls in the poem is described as a 'bosomy English rose'. This makes her seem both voluptuous and homely. The phrase 'wild oats' is synonymous with sexual activity.
- 'Afternoons' — the tree gradually shedding its leaves is used as an image for the fading afternoon and dwindling life.

Extremity and endings

In 'Here', Larkin explores the extremities of land and sea. Hull is described as 'terminate', and the traveller proceeding beyond it comes to 'Isolate villages' and then the coast. This progress seems spiritual, as if in reaching the end of the land the traveller also approaches the end of experience.

'Faith Healing' explores the profound influence of the healing service on the women who attend it, suggesting that it puts an end to their 'sense of life lived according to love' and leads to deep dissatisfaction and an 'immense slackening ache'. 'An Arundel Tomb' again addresses the end of life and love, questioning the veracity of the enduring image of fidelity the tomb presents: 'Time has transfigured them into/Untruth.' 'MCMXIV' captures the end of an era and the loss of innocence attendant on the coming of the First World War.

Colour

Poets conventionally use colour in a symbolic way (e.g. red to connote danger or green to imply jealousy). Larkin uses it as a way of representing the transition from the drabness and absence of colour of the postwar years (see 'Mr Bleaney') to the bright visual contrast of the 1960s, with its psychedelic art and mass-produced clothing.

Examples of Larkin's use of colour and the effects it achieves are given in the table below. It also features in a non-specific way in 'Love Songs in Age', where the daughter's colouring of one of the musical manuscripts becomes a sign of life and a good memory from the past, and in 'Naturally the Foundation will Bear your Expenses', in which the traveller comments on the absence of colour in the 'colourless and careworn' crowd that halts the progress of his taxi along Whitehall.

Colour	Poems	Impact and connotations
silver	'Faith Healing'	age respectability
	'Essential Beauty'	wealth opulence
white	'Ambulances'	illness fear
	'Faith Healing'	innocence naivety
	'Sunny Prestatyn'	alluring, virginal
	'Essential Beauty'	wealth

Colour	Poems	Impact and connotations
'lemons, mauves, and olive-ochres'	'The Whitsun Weddings'	liveliness brightness separation tastelessness? garishness? modernity syntheticness
'browns and greys, maroon and navy' 'Lemon, sapphire, moss-green, rose'	'The Large Cool Store'	choice variety vibrancy modernity syntheticness
yellow	'A Study of Reading Habits'	jaundice unhealthiness cowardice
black	'Dockery and Son'	mourning death
golden	'Essential Beauty'	richness decadence
grey	'Ambulances'	indefiniteness uncertainty
red	'Ambulances'	blood danger

Opposites

The prevalence of opposites in *The Whitsun Weddings* conveys Larkin's sense of living on the cusp between two ages and between social classes. He could see both forwards and backwards, and seemed to live a double life, being respectable and yet outrageous. He saw marriage, advertising and even ambulances as delusions offering hope and happiness, but really peddling frustration and despair, health masquerading as death. This would explain the ambivalence, paradoxes and use of oxymorons prevalent in his work.

Rural/urban

Larkin evokes the rural world of the farm in 'First Sight' to convey his message of the harshness of existence facing the newborn lamb, but the poem also strikes a hopeful note as it anticipates the arrival of spring. Urban environments are portrayed in 'Naturally the Foundation will Bear your Expenses' and 'For Sidney Bechet'. In the former, two huge cities, London and Bombay, are featured, and the pressures, frustrations and busyness of London life are evoked in the crowds. Sidney Bechet's trumpet conjures up an image of the city of New Orleans. The 'legendary Quarter' with its 'balconies, flower-baskets and quadrilles' is romantically idealised.

Frequently Larkin includes both the rural and the urban within a poem. Stanzas 1 and 4 of 'Here' deal mainly with the rural (the Holderness), while stanzas 2 and 3 focus largely on the urban (Hull). Larkin emphasises the liberating qualities of 'solitude' and 'Loneliness', which provide access to 'unfenced existence'. The city, by contrast, is a bustle of activity and consumerist desire. It is 'terminate', implying that it is a dead end (which, geographically, Hull is), and 'mortgaged', further suggesting the restrictions of urban life. In 'Dockery and Son', the open and idyllic spaces of the Oxford college ('The lawn spreads dazzlingly wide') are starkly contrasted to 'the fumes/And furnace-glares of Sheffield'.

'Nothing to be Said' contrasts rural and urban people and their ways of life as a means of exploring the common lot of humanity and, in Larkin's view, the ultimate meaningless of life. In 'MCMXIV', both the urban ('The Oval or Villa Park') and the rural ('the countryside not caring') stand in ignorance of the coming horror of the First World War.

Noise and silence

- 'Here' — the poem moves from silence to the hum of the big city and then on into silence again. Silence particularly characterises the final stanza, where 'silence stands/Like heat' and where the persona comes to terms with 'unfenced existence:/Facing the sun, untalkative, out of reach'.
- 'Mr Bleaney' — the persona of the poem, in his new rooms, finds himself 'Stuffing my ears with cotton-wool, to drown/The jabbering set he egged her on to buy'.
- 'Faith Healing' — after the ministrations of the faith healer, some of the women 'go in silence', but 'some stay stiff, twitching and loud/With deep hoarse tears, as if a kind of dumb/And idiot child within them still survives'.
- 'For Sidney Bechet' — contrasting to the sound of the music, we find 'Mute glorious Storyvilles'.
- 'The Whitsun Weddings' — the quietness of the at first empty train is gradually broken by the weddings encountered ('At first, I didn't notice what a noise/The weddings made'), a picture built upon with 'mothers loud and fat;/An uncle shouting smut' and the noise suggested when the 'last confetti and advice were thrown'. This is followed by the silence of the remainder of the journey to London.

Fast and slow

- 'Here' — in the first stanza Larkin invokes 'the widening river's slow presence', an image that contrasts with the vibrancy and pace of the city.
- 'Naturally the Foundation will Bear your Expenses' — the poem commences with vocabulary conveying speed: 'Hurrying', 'Comet', 'snatch'. By contrast, progress is delayed in Whitehall by a traffic jam and once the persona is airborne decreased movement is suggested by the word 'dwindle'.

- 'Faith Healing' — the nervousness and reverence of the women at the healing service are displayed in their movement: 'Slowly the women file to where he stands'. Their slowness (perhaps hesitancy) contrasts with the incisive and quick movements of the healer, who 'scarcely pausing, goes into a prayer' and clasps their heads 'abruptly'. The realisation in the third stanza, however, is ambiguous: its onset is speedy (it 'sweeps'), but it leaves 'An immense slackening ache'.
- 'The Whitsun Weddings' — the poem opens with 'all sense/Of being in a hurry gone' and the train's journey describes 'A slow and stopping curve southwards'. After the train has gathered its load of newlyweds, however, it 'hurried towards London, shuffling gouts of steam', gathering speed and impetus, until in the final stanza, in which the arrow imagery implies speed, it 'raced across/Bright knots of rail' and 'slowed again' to enter the terminus.

Young and old, past and present

- 'Love Songs in Age' — this is a poem that considers the effect of age on memories of love. The old woman, reflecting on her life and marriage, re-evaluates her younger self; 'the unfailing sense of being young' and the assumptions and certainties that went with youth are no longer with her. She comes to realise that the 'love' she has based her life on is hollow.
- 'The Whitsun Weddings' — this poem contrasts the hope and excitement of the newlyweds and the young people present with the more experienced relatives at the wedding, who understand the 'religious wounding' and all its implications.
- 'MCMXIV' — here Larkin is dealing not so much with old and young people as with an old and a young culture. The 'moustached archaic faces' and the 'dark-clothed children at play' are symbols of an old world, a world of innocence and hope prior to the First World War that could not last and can never be repeated.
- 'First Sight' — the newborn lambs' innocence and fragility is contrasted with the more experienced, wise and weary ewe.
- 'Dockery and Son' — age is important from the outset: '"Dockery was junior to you,/Wasn't he?"' The poem explores the returning student's memory of his Oxford past and causes him to compare his maturity to his youth. He is led by the presence of Dockery's son at the funeral to compare his own youth with that of Dockery, and to consider the different values and needs they had, especially Dockery's need to procreate. The persona of the poem is surprised by the young age at which Dockery felt this need, which he has never felt himself.
- 'An Arundel Tomb' — the ancient tomb embodies a past age ('jointed armour', 'the pre-baroque', 'the old tenantry', 'blazon'), but also eternal issues and values. This is summed up in the concept of the 'stationary voyage', which transcends time, passing on into our own 'unarmorial age'.

Isolation and connection

- 'Here' — in this poem, isolation brings the narrator into a true form of contact with himself. Passing through the bustle and noise of Hull on to the Holderness peninsula, past 'Isolate villages' and the 'removed lives' of their inhabitants, he finds himself almost spiritually elevated and engaged by the experience. This is conveyed by the statement 'Loneliness clarifies'.
- 'The Whitsun Weddings' — the narrator moves from the isolation of the 'three-quarters-empty train' to the connection of a significant shared experience with the newly married couples that join the train as it heads south towards London.
- 'The Importance of Elsewhere' — being an outsider in Ireland affords the persona a certain freedom that would not be allowed to a native: in England no excuse of foreignness 'underwrites my existence'. Newness and separation provide their own strange comfort: to the narrator of the poem 'Strangeness made sense', and in his 'difference' he feels 'welcome' as he finds himself 'separate, not unworkable'.

Freedom and constraint

- 'Here' — with its retailers and businesses, its 'raw estates' and 'dead straight miles', the city seems constrained, whereas the Holderness peninsula that lies towards the sea offers 'unfenced existence': no limits, openness and freedom.
- 'Mr Bleaney' — although he is a single man (compare 'Self's the Man' and 'Dockery and Son'), traditionally an image of freedom and carefree existence, Mr Bleaney's life and the 'one hired box' that encapsulates it seem decidedly constrained.
- 'Love Songs in Age' — the memories of the past and past love that the widow recalls seem like a self-deluding and comforting prison that it is too painful for her to escape from.
- 'Self's the Man' and 'Dockery and Son' — both poems question whether marriage and singleness offer freedom or constraint. The answer seems to be that it depends upon the individuals, their circumstances and their preferences — each can be either stultifying or liberating.

Life and death

- 'Love Songs in Age' — this poem deals with the life and death of love and also the life and death of self-delusion in the ageing woman, as she realises the truth of what her 'love' actually was.
- 'Take One Home for the Kiddies' — the darkly comic **juxtaposition** of the life and death of the animals points out the fragility of life and the closeness of the states of life and death.
- 'Ambulances' — the poem operates around the stark contrast of the healthy (i.e. life) and the ill (i.e. death). The fearful relationship between the two states is illustrated in the response of the healthy to the unwell.

- 'Dockery and Son' — the poem begins with a funeral. As it proceeds, it explores the need to mask the inevitability of death and extinction by procreation, as if children become an extension of the self.

Marriage and singleness

- 'The Whitsun Weddings' — this poem uses the language of weddings and the ceremony that surrounds them ('an event', 'confetti', descriptions of the wedding guests and their clothes, 'a happy funeral'), though sometimes in an indirect and obscure way ('religious wounding', 'being changed'). This gives the poem an air of uncertainty alongside its sense of celebration.
- 'Self's the Man' — the single man is isolated, having no wife or 'nippers', but seems very happy with this, comparing himself favourably to his friend Arnold, whose life he sees as a constraining round of duties.

Truth and deception

Many of the poems in *The Whitsun Weddings* deal with honesty and dishonesty:

- 'An Arundel Tomb' — Larkin considers the extent to which the carved image on the tomb conveys a true impression of the couple's relationship. Much hinges on the 'sharp tender shock' of the couple's clasped hands, a detail added at a later stage to the original monument, and therefore deceptive and misleading. The monument is 'sweet commissioned grace', which alerts us to the fact that it may 'sweeten' the reality of their relationship. The issue of deception is most starkly portrayed in the final stanza: 'Time has transfigured them into/Untruth.' The poem does not, however, hide our desire for truth ('to prove/Our almost-instinct almost true') and the comfort such security brings.
- 'Talking in Bed' — lying together in bed is at first presented as 'An emblem of two people being honest'. However, the relationship changes as the couple take refuge in silence, struggling 'to find/Words at once true and kind,/Or not untrue and not unkind'.
- 'Essential Beauty' — this poem addresses the issue of advertising. Larkin contrasts the deceptive promises of glossy advertisements (e.g. 'A glass of milk stands in a meadow') with reality. Structurally the poem reflects this contrast; the first stanza is idealistic (deceptive), and the second is realistic (truthful). The brightness of the vocabulary in the first stanza (praise, shine, fine, radiant, warm) contrasts with the harshness and dullness of stanza 2 (coldness, dark, puking, dying, dappled). The inextricable connection between truth and deception is neatly conveyed in the use of **enjambement** to link the two stanzas, where Larkin observes how the advertisements 'Reflect none of the rained-on streets and squares//They dominate outdoors'.

- 'Send No Money' — this poem holds the notion of truth as a concept up to scrutiny. The persona is searching for truth, but the initial image of 'the fobbed/ Impendent belly of Time' suggests that truth may be an undesirable illusion. The second stanza links truth with the blows of personal experience, an uncomforting and uncompromising reality. This is summed up in the final judgement that truth is a 'trite untransferable/Truss-advertisement'.

Corporeal and abstract

In *The Whitsun Weddings* tangible objects often provide the starting point for reflections on issues of a more transcendental nature. Items such as clothes, bodies and consumer products are set alongside abstract concepts such as air, light, emotions, memory and music. Key examples occur in the following poems:

- 'Here' — the buildings ('statues, spires and cranes', 'mortgaged half-built edges' of the city) and consumer objects ('Cheap suits, red kitchen-ware, sharp shoes, iced lollies,/Electric mixers, toasters, washers, driers') which represent Hull provide a stark contrast to the abstract 'loneliness', 'luminously-peopled air' and 'unfenced existence' of the Holderness. The constrained definition of the city contrasts with the liberating freedom of the peninsula.
- 'Mr Bleaney' — objects such as the 'Flowered curtains, thin and frayed', 'Bed, upright chair, sixty-watt bulb' and 'saucer-souvenir' define the spartan existence of Mr Bleaney, and pave the way for an abstract consideration of 'dread' and the meaning of life, questioning whether possessions and the lodgings we inhabit are fair reflections of 'our own nature'.
- 'Love Songs in Age' — the sheet music for the love songs of the title moves the reader towards the abstract issue of love itself. The sheet music becomes a metaphor for love ('each frank submissive chord/Had ushered in/Word after sprawling hyphenated word'), which, like the music, too painful for contemplation, must be hidden away.
- 'Broadcast' — the abstract wavebands or radio waves transmit music, emotion and a clear impression of the beloved's physicality. Listening at a distance, the lover re-creates a sense of the 'face among all those faces', 'gloves', 'slightly-outmoded shoes' and the 'hands' of his beloved.
- 'The Importance of Elsewhere' — the sights, smells and sounds of the fishing port provide a starting point for Larkin's philosophical reflections on the nature of belonging and the security of being an outsider.

Light and dark

Images of light and dark appear in almost every poem in the collection. Traditionally, light is associated with good and dark with evil. However, Larkin employs light and dark to achieve a wide range of effects:

- 'Here' — the 'industrial shadows' of the northward journey give way to the brightness of Hull and its surroundings. The vocabulary of light takes over to express Larkin's love of his adopted home and its environs: 'shining gull-marked mud', 'luminously-peopled air', 'sun'.
- 'Water' — the poem ends with the striking image of endless 'any-angled light'. This is an image full of promise and wealth, suggesting the powerful spirituality that underlies Larkin's view of the world.
- 'The Whitsun Weddings' — Larkin carefully contrasts light and dark, as befits a poem about the 'happy funeral' that is a wedding. The 'bright summer afternoon' and the 'Bright knots of rail' are balanced by 'long shadows' and 'walls of blackened moss' as the train approaches London and the couples' married futures.
- 'MCMXIV' — the use of light and dark in this poem reflects the sense of naive hope felt by the nation in the face of oncoming war. The heady heat of an idealised English summer is suggested by 'sun' and 'sunblinds', but 'Shadowing Domesday lines' could be said to presage the trenches.
- 'Essential Beauty' — the deceptive advertisements that are the subject of the poem use images of light: 'fine/Midsummer weather', 'radiant bars/(Gas or electric)' and 'white-clothed ones'. These are contrasted with the 'dark-raftered pubs', 'No match lit up' and 'going dark' of reality.

Humour

Larkin's poetry often includes black and satirical humour. It is rarely straightforwardly funny, and often shocking and discomforting. Poems where this is particularly evident, and examples of their humour, are given below.

'Naturally the Foundation will Bear your Expenses'

- The rhythm is tripping and witty.
- Trite rhymes are included (e.g. Comet/from it; Professor Lal/my pal), which create a satirical tone.
- The references are over-familiar (e.g. 'Morgan Forster' for the novelist E. M. Forster, who wrote *A Passage to India*).
- Playing on the title of Forster's novel, Larkin presents us with a passage to India.
- The second stanza is full of mock solemnity, with the pageantry of the Whitehall Remembrance parade.

'Take One Home for the Kiddies'

- The voices of the children, their sense that this is just a game, and the presentation of the death of the animals ('Fetch the shoebox, fetch the shovel'), are examples of **black humour**.

- The tone is one of mock-**pathos**.
- The poem offers a dispassionate view of death.
- The animals are 'Living toys'.

'Toads Revisited'
- The final image of the man walking arm-in-arm with the toad is humorous.
- The poem includes comic **stereotypes** (e.g. 'Palsied old step-takers,/Hare-eyed clerks with the jitters').
- 'Cemetery Road' is an example of **black humour**.

'As Bad as a Mile'
- The reversal of events is amusing.
- The apple core is a comic source of poetry.

'A Study of Reading Habits'
- The language is **colloquial**.
- The readers are stereotypes.
- In the third stanza, fictional stereotypes are debunked.
- In the second stanza there is black humour in the disturbing images.

'Sunny Prestatyn'
- '*Titch Thomas*' contrasts with the 'tuberous cock and balls'.
- The language is scurrilous.
- The light-hearted tone of the poem's opening becomes black, and the humour is disturbingly sexual by its end.

The key poems

'Here'

In this poem Larkin evokes Hull, his adopted home for many years. The poet loved the remoteness of the place: 'I like it because it's so far from everywhere else' (*Required Writing*, p. 54). Hull was changing by the time Larkin arrived there in 1955. It retained something of its old fish-port history (and odour) — as the poem celebrates — but was also looking towards a new and undefined future. As Andrew Motion writes in his 1993 biography of Larkin:

> What Larkin found...was a city at the end of one kind of life, waiting for another to begin. Wandering along the wooden cobbles of the deserted high street in the Old Town, past the disintegrating warehouses and sunken boats rotting in inland docks, he felt he was in a place set on the edge of things. Isolated on the hook of

> land that forms the north shore of the Humber, on the way to nowhere except the North Sea, it felt particular, intriguing and remote.
>
> (*Philip Larkin: A Writer's Life*, p. 249)

In fact, the city and the nearby Holderness embodied all that Larkin was at the time and largely remained for the whole of his writing life.

Opposites

The construction of opposites is a central technique in *The Whitsun Weddings* and a number of examples can be found in 'Here'. They create a sense of separation, difference, remoteness and isolation which goes beyond geography to acquire spiritual associations:

- Crowds/isolation, e.g. 'cut-price crowds', 'Isolate villages'; for Larkin, crowds can be as lonely as isolation.
- Swerve/straight, e.g. 'Swerving east', 'The dead straight miles'; curves suggest ease and liberation, while straightness implies a clinical, impersonally purposeful movement.
- North/east — movement north in the poem is characterised by bustle and frenetic energy, whereas the move to the east, to Hull and then beyond to the Holderness, is associated with relaxation and peace.
- Urban/rural — while the poem displays an obvious affection for the city of Hull, true release and discovery is only found in rural spaces.
- Movement/stillness — the movement of traffic and the city is contrasted with the stillness of the rural environment, and the Holderness in particular.

Consumerism

Consumerism is an issue that emerges regularly throughout Larkin's work. This interest is especially apparent in stanzas 2 and 3 of 'Here'. The urban heart of Hull is characterised by its businesses and shops and the crowds who 'Push through plate-glass swing doors to their desires —/Cheap suits, red kitchen-ware, sharp shoes, iced lollies,/Electric mixers, toasters, washers, driers'. This list is a comment on the new convenience culture and its tendency towards the tangible and away from the intangible. The populous urban environment provides a contrast with the rural landscape and the relaxed pace of life of the Holderness. The definite, clear-cut, branded nature of the consumer culture contrasts strikingly with the numinous location (beyond the needs of such definition) in which the poem ends.

Larkin paints a multifarious, vivid and almost affectionate portrait of the city. It has a maritime history, as the reference to 'the slave museum,/Tattoo-shops, consulates' indicates; its association with the slave trade points to a particularly dark and distasteful element of Hull's past. There is an ongoing maritime economy ('barge-crowded water'; 'ships up streets'; 'fishy-smelling'). It is an isolated place, distanced from the 'traffic all night north', and unexpected: 'Gathers to the surprise of a large town'. The city is at the end of the line ('terminate'), suggesting isolation, extremity and dead-endedness. Hull seems big and impersonal (the descriptions of the bustling crowds of shoppers), and yet curiously intimate ('fishy-smelling/Pastoral of ships up streets'). The city is expanding ('cranes cluster'; 'mortgaged half-built edges'), but it has civic grandeur ('domes and statues, spires') and in parts a primitive, old-worldly quality ('grain-scattered streets'). However, there are suggestions of a harsh existence ('grim head-scarfed wives'). There is a stark juxtaposition of the rural and the urban (the town comes as a 'surprise'), and the peninsula beyond offers an uplifting experience of release and escape.

Lists

Throughout 'Here' Larkin makes use of lists. These maintain the momentum of the poem, especially through the expansive first sentence, and create variations in pace. In stanza 1, the list of rural scenes through which the train is 'Swerving' creates steady momentum and builds up towards the 'surprise' of the large town. Larkin gains a rhythmic effect through the use of **alliterative** pairs of words (e.g. 'harsh-named halt'; 'skies and scarecrows'; 'haystacks, hares'; 'gull-marked mud'). A faster pace is created in stanza 2 as Larkin lists details of the city which conjure up a vivid sense of its atmosphere. This serves to balance the list of rural images in stanza 1, a fact emphasised by the use he again makes of alliterative pairs (e.g. 'statues, spires'; 'cranes cluster'; 'grain-scattered streets'; 'residents from raw estates'). The listing of scenes and landmarks in stanza 3 opens up perspectives on the city's appearance, geography, history, culture and economy (e.g. 'ships up streets, the slave museum'; 'mortgaged half-built edges').

Loneliness and freedom

'Here' ends with the persona moving beyond the city out onto the Holderness peninsula. As 'Loneliness clarifies', he reflects on the need for 'unfenced existence'. This combination of loneliness and freedom has a number of effects. It generates life ('weeds flower'; 'waters quicken'); it provides anonymity ('Here leaves unnoticed thicken'); it offers neutrality and space ('bluish neutral distance'); and it brings light ('Luminously-peopled'; 'sun'), suggesting spiritual enlightenment, or an epiphany.

This is comparable to 'The Importance of Elsewhere'. As in 'Here', it is physical remoteness that leads to clarity of vision. The differences between the persona of the poem and his adopted Irish neighbours are significant, as are the differences between the traveller and the people of Hull in 'Here'. In each case it is the feeling of isolation that helps create definition and a fuller sense of self. Distance from the familiar and the customary is essential; this does not provide the insecurity that we might expect, but on the contrary a certain security in freedom, an insurance that 'underwrites' existence available only to the outsider.

'Mr Bleaney'

In his biography of Larkin, Andrew Motion describes the succession of bedsits and flats that the poet–librarian inhabited throughout the majority of his life. Typical of Larkin's descriptions that Motion quotes are the following:

> I cannot give you much of a picture of my room. It is a medium-sized attic, with carpet and bed, and I sit in a basket chair by a reading lamp with an electric radiator pointed cunningly up my arse and a brown rug over my shoulders.
>
> (Letter to Jim Sutton, 30 September 1946)

> I am established in an attic with a small window, a bed, an armchair, a basket chair, a carpet, a reading lamp THAT DOESN'T WORK, a small electric fire THAT DOESN'T WORK and a few books, papers, etc.
>
> (Letter to Kingsley Amis, 30 September 1946)

At the time he wrote these letters, Larkin had recently completed his degree at Oxford and was commencing work as a librarian in Leicester. There is therefore a class difference and a physical/intellectual dichotomy between the persona and Mr Bleaney, as the persona is based on Larkin's own experiences.

There are a number of clear and instructive parallels between these descriptions and the world of 'Mr Bleaney'. The details in the sources and the poem are similar — 'Bed, upright chair, sixty-watt bulb, no hook/Behind the door' — and build the impression of a soulless, dispiriting place. Both the poem and the quotations demonstrate Larkin's bleak sense of humour at work, e.g. the strategically placed radiator in the first extract and the persona's knowledge of Mr Bleaney's habits in the poem. However, in Mr Bleaney's room there is 'no room for books'; in Larkin's room there is a reading lamp (although it doesn't work) and some books and papers, reflecting the vital place of literature in Larkin's world. The lack of culture in Mr Bleaney's life may reflect his class — he works at the 'Bodies', the body workshop of the Cowley car plant in Oxford, whereas Larkin was from a middle-class, educated background.

The single man

'Mr Bleaney' is about the life of the single man, and can be compared to 'Self's the Man' and 'Dockery and Son'. The poem questions the value of the single life; if our nature is measured by 'how we live', what does this say about Mr Bleaney and others like him? A strong sense of the bleakness of Mr Bleaney's existence emerges:

- He is isolated — he doesn't seem to have any deep relationships.
- Routine is important in his life, with the mundane round of work and hoping for 'the four aways' (i.e. doing the football pools, hoping for away wins) and annual rituals of Christmas with his sister and a seaside holiday in Frinton.
- Gardening is a lonely activity for him.

- His chats with his landlady suggest he has no one closer to talk to.
- The phrase 'one hired box' suggested a limited existence, and a coffin.
- The 'five inches' of life Mr Bleaney can see from his window suggests his narrow existence.
- The idea that Mr Bleaney's room can be considered a 'home' is incongruous.
- The name Mr Bleaney, with its long vowels, suggests bleakness and boredom.

The persona presents a wryly funny and at the same time pathetic picture of Mr Bleaney's life, but the humorous and somewhat dismissive tone can obscure the similarity between the persona and the man whose existence he is summarising. In reality they have much in common, as both of their lives are defined by 'one hired box'. However, the last two stanzas suggest that whereas Mr Bleaney found sources of security and satisfaction in his circumscribed existence, the persona is prey to dread and doubt about what his life amounts to.

Everyday objects

There are several everyday objects mentioned in the poem that create an impression of limitation and boredom. The impersonality and utilitarian functionality of the lodgings is conveyed by the inventory Larkin gives in stanzas 2–3. The curtains are 'thin and frayed', suggesting an impoverished and weary existence; they do not cover the whole window, and this inadequacy can be extended by association to the room, its occupants and their way of life. The television set (Andrew Motion believes it to be a radio set) emphasises the difference between Mr Bleaney and his successor. Mr Bleaney, unlike the persona, had no baggage and was not a reader; these are basic lodgings where cheapness is everything, as symbolised by the 60-watt bulb (too weak for reading).

Comparison with 'Home is so Sad'

The close focus on Mr Bleaney's room bears obvious resemblances to 'Home is so Sad', in terms of both place and atmosphere:

- Mr Bleaney's 'hired box' is a bleak, empty and impersonal place, whereas the home in 'Home is so Sad' has decorative objects and personal touches: the 'pictures and the cutlery./The music in the piano stool. That vase.'
- Both poems employ flower imagery: in 'Mr Bleaney' the frayed curtains have a flowered pattern, like a tired mockery of life, while in 'Home is so Sad' the forlorn home 'withers' in the absence of its inhabitants.
- The relationship between the home and the inhabitant is explored in both poems: in 'Mr Bleaney' home seems to define the man, whereas in 'Home is so Sad' the absent inhabitant seems to define the home.
- Both homes seem, for different reasons, spiritless: Mr Bleaney's room because it was never the personal, comfortable backdrop to loving relationships; the home

in 'Home is so Sad' because there is no longer 'anyone to please' and because the ideal it started as (the 'joyous shot at how things ought to be') has not lasted.

'The Whitsun Weddings'

In an interview in 1981 with Melvyn Bragg for the *South Bank Show*, Larkin offered an explanation of the genesis of 'The Whitsun Weddings', an experience on Whit Saturday, 1955:

> [I caught] a very slow train that stopped at every station and I hadn't realised that, of course, this was the train that all the wedding couples would get on and go to London for their honeymoon[;] it was an eye-opener to me. Every party was different but the same somehow. They all looked different but they were all doing the same things and sort of feeling the same things. I suppose the train stopped at about four, five, six stations between Hull and London and there was a sense of gathering emotional momentum. Every time you stopped fresh emotion climbed aboard. And finally between Peterborough and London when you hurtle on, you felt the whole thing was being aimed like a bullet — at the heart of things, you know. All this fresh, open life. Incredible experience. I've never forgotten it.

As the title poem of the volume, this is obviously one of the key texts in *The Whitsun Weddings*.

Marriage

Larkin employs the language of weddings and the ceremony that surrounds them throughout 'The Whitsun Weddings'. Although he was strongly opposed to marriage, the prevailing mood of the poem is warm, even celebratory. As the persona describes the families crowded onto railway platforms at the end of the day to see the newlyweds off on their honeymoons, it is hard to avoid the magnetism of the shared experience.

However, other emotions are also present. The persona retains his distance as an interested voyeur, an outsider evaluating what he sees. The language of weddings often seems tangential and even disembodied, as if consciously unwilling to engage fully in the happiness of the event. Advice, for example, is thrown like confetti, suggesting its ephemeral and fragile nature and illustrating Larkin's cynicism. Contrast lies at the heart of marriage: joining and parting; innocence and experience; happiness and sadness; beginning and ending. This is evident in the use of **oxymoron** ('a happy funeral', 'religious wounding') and in the pervading sense that nothing can be the same after this day, that it involves 'being changed' fundamentally. This gives the poem an air of uncertainty alongside its sense of celebration. It is hard not to see the final image of the falling arrow-shower as a forewarning of the difficulties of marriage explored elsewhere in the collection, such as the experiences of Arnold and his wife in 'Self's the Man' or the nameless couples of 'Afternoons'.

The poem offers a number of perspectives on marriage. These are as follows:

- 'an event' — the traveller describes the wedding in dispassionate and distant terms, at a remove from personal engagement
- 'Success so huge and wholly farcical' — this captures the fathers' ridiculous but understandable pride in their children's marriage
- 'something dull' — to the children it is a long and boring day with ageing and distant relatives, something to which they cannot yet relate
- 'a religious wounding' — for the girls the excitement (and fear) of sexual intercourse is at the heart of their response to marriage
- 'a happy funeral' — for the older women, who know both the good and the bad points about their own marriages, the combination of the positive and the negative is important

Journeys

The metaphor of the journey, a common literary device to represent life, is significant to this poem. On one level the poem can be read as a literal description of a journey from Hull to London, but it clearly has important symbolic overtones. The journey is one of enlightenment for the traveller, the newlyweds and the reader. It becomes a significant life experience (maybe even a life-changing experience), as Larkin indicates in the final stanza, when he refers to 'all the power/That being changed can give'. He exploits this **pun** on the railway 'change' in 'Dockery and Son' too. The journey involves leave-taking (from the past, from families, from the single state) as well as an adventure into new realms (of marriage); the reference to 'religious wounding' suggests the journey from sexual innocence to sexual experience. However, the phrase 'this frail/Travelling coincidence' suggests that the journey of marriage may be fragile, and the reader is forced to question whether this is a journey into liberty ('Free at last') or constraint ('the tightened brakes took hold').

Imagery

Railways

Several of Larkin's concerns are connected to his use of railways in the poem. Solitude is evident in the 'three-quarters-empty train', and pleasure, relaxation and leisurely progress are evoked by the lines 'All windows down, all cushions hot, all sense/Of being in a hurry gone'. The sensory nature of the experience is emphasised by phrases such as 'the reek of buttoned carriage-cloth', 'the long cool platforms' and 'shuffling gouts of steam'. The literal journey from Hull to London comes to symbolise the journeys of life and of marriage, the latter having just begun for all the travelling couples. Similarly, the criss-crossing rails ('Bright knots of rail') are an image of intersection, the crossing of paths and temporary meetings; the phrase 'this frail/Travelling coincidence' further suggests this.

Arrows

The image of an 'arrow-shower', used in the final stanza, is ambiguous. Its association with rain could make it seem to be an image of refreshment and renewal. However, the image is sharp and threatening as well; the danger represented by the arrows cannot be overlooked. The uncertainty attached to the image in the phrase 'Sent out of sight' is disconcerting, suggesting unknown outcomes and destinations. Firing arrows at clouds is a Native American rain-making ritual, and suggests the desire/need for rain. The railway lines converging on London suggest arrows fired at a target.

Elements

The sun is the predominant meteorological image in the poem, creating a prevailingly positive view appropriate to a wedding day: 'sun destroys/The interest of what's happening in the shade'. Rain enters the poem in the last line, however, darkening the tone. Note the use of all four elements in stanza 1 — fire (sun), air (sky), water (river) and earth (Lincolnshire) — which creates a sense of balance and completion.

Opposites

Throughout the poem Larkin evokes opposites, pointing to the contrast that lies at the heart of marriage.

Rural and urban

Reversing the dynamic of 'Here', this poem begins and ends in the city. The journey is from Hull to London, passing through large areas of countryside, as well as other towns, on the way. The urban 'backs of houses' and 'blinding windscreens' of stanza 1 are in contrast to the rural 'tall heat' and 'Wide farms' of stanza 2. The transition from a rural to an urban landscape is captured by the use of the term 'acres' in the description of a scrap yard: 'the next town, new and nondescript,/ Approached with acres of dismantled cars.' Pastoral language is applied to the metropolis elsewhere, too, for example in the simile, 'London spread out in the sun,/Its postal districts packed like squares of wheat'.

Expectation and disappointment

- 'Success so huge and wholly farcical' — this encapsulates the ridiculous pride of the fathers
- 'each face seemed to define/Just what it saw departing' — there is a bittersweet sense of gain and loss as the train pulls away
- 'happy funeral'; 'religious wounding' — use of oxymoron to clarify mixed emotions

Motion and stillness

This clearly links with the poem's use of travel as a metaphor:

- 'We ran/Behind the backs of houses' — the poem opens with an easy pace
- 'Each station that we stopped at' — routine stillness punctuates the momentum of the poem
- 'whoops and skirls' — this suggests frenetic, excited movement
- 'We passed them' — the characters are beginning a journey that takes them beyond the people at the station
- 'posed irresolutely' — the uncertain stillness suggests nervousness and hesitation
- 'Fresh couples climbed aboard: the rest stood round' — the contrast between the movement of the newlyweds and the stasis of the onlookers is striking
- 'We hurried towards London' — Larkin is building up towards the climax of the poem
- 'A dozen marriages got under way' — this links the marriages to trains and journeys, as the train itself starts to gain momentum

Breadth and narrowness

The contrast between the spacious and the constrained is particularly relevant to a poem focusing on marriage and suggests Larkin's ambiguous views. Key examples include:

- 'The river's level drifting breadth began'
- 'Wide farms went by'
- 'long cool platforms'
- 'London spread out in the sun'
- 'walls of blackened moss/Came close'
- 'the tightened brakes took hold'

Height and shortness

- 'tall heat' — the heat does not seem oppressive, but contributes to the atmosphere of ease and tranquillity
- 'short-shadowed cattle' — this evokes summer by conveying that the sun is high in the sky
- 'poplars cast/Long shadows' — the shadows cast by the trees provide an ambiguous image: they may be a comforting shade, or they may suggest a darkening landscape, especially as they follow another phrase which indicates a transition to a less open environment: 'Now fields were building-plots'

Togetherness and separation

Marriages involve both union and separation: union with a new husband or wife and separation from parents. Key examples include:

- the colours of their dresses 'Marked off the girls unreally from the rest', and this line is separated by a stanza break

- 'Where sky and Lincolnshire and water meet' — this suggests the coming together of different elements, like man and wife in the wedding service
- the families at the stations stand 'As if out on the end of an event/Waving goodbye' — this captures both involvement and marginalisation
- 'the wedding-days/Were coming to an end' — this conveys both the beginnings and the endings represented by marriage
- 'each face seemed to define/Just what it saw departing' — this suggests that marriage leads not only to gain, but also to loss
- 'none/Thought of the others they would never meet/Or how their lives would all contain this hour' — this conjures up both a defining moment of togetherness and captures the isolation and self-absorption of each newlywed couple, as well as detachment from the observer

Ends and beginnings

- The day of the wedding and the ceremony itself is both an end and a beginning. It is the end of singleness and the start of the new couple's life together. For Larkin it would symbolise the end of freedom and the beginning of the imprisonment of marriage (compare 'Self's the Man' and 'Afternoons').
- Marriage, with its inevitable 'religious wounding', represents the end of virginity.
- The oxymoron 'happy funeral' is applied to the weddings the persona sees. This incongruous image implies that death (or ending) is implicit in the very beginnings of marriage.
- Marriage symbolises the start of a new generation, the passing on of responsibility and experience from one generation to the next.
- The poem traces a journey from its beginning in Hull to its terminus in London. The train journey is a metaphor for the lives and marriages the persona encounters.

Women

Many of the poems in the collection give a single perspective on women, but 'The Whitsun Weddings' offers a proliferation of views. This helps differentiate the various responses women have to the issue of marriage and all that it entails:

- Girls are separated from the older women and are literally made to stand out from the crowd by the bold, bright clothes that mark them off 'unreally from the rest' — the use of the word 'unreally' suggests false distinction or something unnatural.
- Sexual excitement or fear is important as we see the girls 'gripping their handbags tighter', contemplating the 'religious wounding' to come.
- Handbags may be seen as a symbol of female private parts.
- The girls are contrasted to the older women; they are bright and silent in the face of marriage, while the mothers are 'loud and fat'.
- The lot of married women is ambiguous: 'The women shared/The secret like a happy funeral'. This suggests a mixed reaction to sex.

Comparison with 'Here'

Both poems use images of straightness and curves; curves seem to represent satisfaction and completion, while straightness seems to be linked to dissatisfaction and incompletion. For example, the 'slow and stopping curve' of 'The Whitsun Weddings' and the opening 'Swerving east' of 'Here' are both pleasant diversions for the poems' personas. Similarly, the 'dead straight miles' of 'Here' and the straight run into London where 'we were arrived' in 'The Whitsun Weddings' carry less positive connotations.

North and south are important in both, though the directions are reversed. The movement north in 'Here' leads to escape and enlightenment, while the movement south in 'The Whitsun Weddings' suggests narrowing and constraint in the experience of marriage. 'The Whitsun Weddings' stops in the city, when it reaches London; 'Here' goes beyond the city of Hull to reach the escape and freedom of the Holderness peninsula.

Both poems deal with 'spiritual' experiences. However, 'Here' ends with a sense of transcendence while 'The Whitsun Weddings' has the word 'somewhere' in its last line; there is a sense of concrete location inherent in this, even if the 'somewhere' is unknown. The full release that ends 'Here' is therefore not achieved in 'The Whitsun Weddings'.

'Dockery and Son'

In *Philip Larkin: A Writer's Life* (1993), Andrew Motion identifies the circumstances in which this poem was composed: 'It describes a visit Larkin had made to his old college at Oxford, St John's, on the way back from the funeral of Agnes Cuming, his predecessor as librarian at Hull' (p. 333).

Railways

The image of the railway plays an important role in this poem, as it does throughout *The Whitsun Weddings*. It suggests journeying; Dockery Senior's journey has now been terminated, while that of the narrator continues, as does that of Dockery's son. The narrator is on a journey of returning to his past as well as going forward to his future. The rails become a metaphor for the intersections and divergences involved in human existence ('the ranged/Joining and parting lines'), but railway travel also evokes solitude — the narrator catches his train 'ignored'.

Exclusion

The persona finds himself excluded in a number of ways, and there is a definite sense of difference and apartness as the poem progresses. He expresses 'the shock/Of finding out how much had gone of life,/How widely from the others' his existence

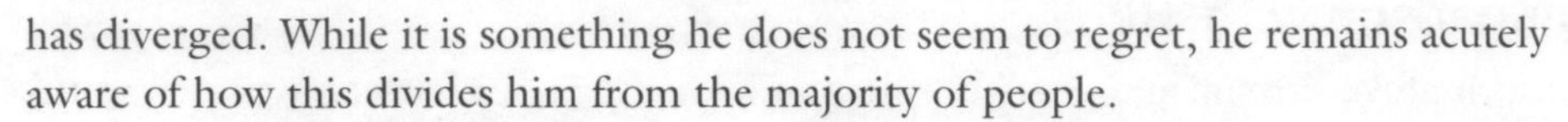

has diverged. While it is something he does not seem to regret, he remains acutely aware of how this divides him from the majority of people.

He is strangely distanced and excluded from his own past and memories of it. The experience is summed up in the pun on 'I changed' (stanza 3). His half-remembered Oxford days are symbolised by the locked door of stanzas 1–2. This image is picked up again in the penultimate stanza, where assumptions 'warp tight-shut, like doors', further excluding him from the world around.

The persona is cut off from memory of exactly who Dockery is: 'Was he that withdrawn//High-collared public-schoolboy, sharing rooms/With Cartwright who was killed?' The ellipses in the poem suggest that the persona is aware that a choice he didn't consciously make has led to this state. The 'club' of fatherhood is shut to him (admittedly through his own choice), and the poem ends with 'the only end of age', death — the ultimate form of exclusion.

Death

The poem seems to begin with the funeral of Dockery Senior, setting the tone for the poem and its focus on death. The changes that the poem traces in the narrator suggest not only physical death, but also the death of the past, the death of memory, and the death of the assumptions upon which life has been based. At the end of the poem the inevitability of death is uncompromisingly stated, although the word 'death' is not used. Reflecting on life, the narrator observes: 'Whether or not we use it, it goes,/And leaves what something hidden from us chose,/And age, and then the only end of age'.

Singleness

Like a number of poems within the collection, 'Dockery and Son' deals with issues of singleness and marriage. Singleness, and the absence of dependants and property, seem 'quite natural' to the persona, who proves ultimately unable to define what Dockery was seeking, or attained, in fathering a son. He imagines that Dockery found his single self inadequate and in need of addition, while the persona believes himself self-sufficient. Dockery needed to 'be added to', while the persona believes relationships and children would serve only as a 'dilution' of his essential and autonomous nature.

Boredom and fear

'Life is first boredom, then fear', states the persona in stanza 6. It could be argued that the persona is essentially bored by the Dean's platitudes: he seems generally unexcited by the memories of his Oxford past and is unable to recall precisely who Dockery was. His half-formed memories bore him — he yawns and falls asleep on the train. The sudden and significant change that occurs at Sheffield demonstrates the shift from boredom to fear: the persona loses his detachment and struggles to define the differences between himself and Dockery, fearing that his 'Innate assumptions' about singleness and children may be wrong. Life and its emptiness are represented as a path to the inevitable 'only end of age', death.

This is a view that can be applied to *The Whitsun Weddings* as a whole. Many of the poems in the volume deal with boredom and fear:

- 'Toads Revisited' looks at the necessary and strangely fulfilling boredom of work.
- 'Love Songs in Age' deals with the routine of marriage and the fear arising from the recognition that love is empty.
- 'Talking in Bed' explores the growth of boredom in a relationship and the fear of causing pain by speaking the truth.
- 'Afternoons' depicts the boring routines of married life and suggests the married couples' fear of finding themselves superseded and marginalised.
- The children in 'Take One Home for the Kiddies' grow bored of their new pets.
- 'Days' is a consummate expression of the boredom allied to fear of the only alternative, death.
- 'Nothing to be Said' traces the inevitable march of slowly advancing time towards death.
- 'Mr Bleaney' outlines the narrow and tedious routines of bedsit existence and reveals the persona's 'dread' that his life is worthless.

However, *The Whitsun Weddings* also offers affirmation (albeit never unqualified) in poems such as 'An Arundel Tomb', 'The Whitsun Weddings', 'Broadcast', 'For Sidney Bechet' and 'First Sight'. These poems explore the more positive emotions and experiences of life.

Language

Ellipses

There are several examples of ellipses in the poem, all of which serve different purposes:

- '"And do/You keep in touch with —"' — the dash here functions in the same way as an ellipsis, to express the Dean's absent-mindedness, the forgettable blandness of his question, or the narrator's straying attention. Any name could follow this cliché. The poem then becomes a **stream of consciousness**.
- 'Well, it just shows/How much...How little...' — this reveals the incomprehension of the narrator and his inability to formulate thought. He is also sleepy at this point.
- 'Dockery, now:/Only nineteen, he must have taken stock/Of what he wanted, and been capable/Of...' — the narrator is unable or unwilling to identify exactly what it is that Dockery wanted and was capable of getting. He is trying to identify what it is that distinguishes Dockery from himself, as is clear from the words with which he cuts off his incomplete meditations: 'No, that's not the difference'.

'Get' and 'got'

The words 'get' and 'got' have two different meanings in the course of the poem:

- to beget children ('did he get this son/At nineteen, twenty?'); Larkin was fascinated by other people's need to have children, something he always personally feared
- to own ('harden into all we've got')

This reflects the poem's concern with the nature of 'getting', in terms of success, possessions and reproduction. Dockery's early reproduction causes the narrator to re-evaluate the nature of what he has 'got' and what he has not.

Family business

The poem's title, 'Dockery and Son', suggests a traditional family business. This offers a number of interesting and helpful angles from which to approach the poem:

- The poem looks at the 'business' of producing children (though this word is not used). It suggests the idea of a family line, which relates to Larkin's use of line imagery elsewhere in the collection.
- The title suggests the idea of legacy and opens to question what is passed on from generation to generation.
- The phrase 'Dockery and Son' encapsulates the relationship between the father and the son: the father is honoured with a name but the son is defined only in relation to the father, and is not assigned his own name or personality.

'An Arundel Tomb'

Larkin composed 'An Arundel Tomb' after a holiday with Monica Jones on the Hampshire coast, in response to seeing a monument to the Earl of Arundel and his wife in a church. The monument struck Larkin forcibly, perhaps reminding him of his own relationship with Monica — a relationship simultaneously marked by its intimacy and its distance. One of the most striking features of the monument for Larkin, and described in the poem, is the joined hands of the earl and his wife — a nineteenth-century addition to the medieval original, as Larkin was later to discover. In the poem he explores his own ambiguous feelings about love and relationships. A note he added at the end of the manuscript draft reads: 'Love isn't stronger than death just because statues hold hands for 600 years.'

Marriage and relationships

At first Larkin's presentation of marriage seems positive; the couple are 'side by side', an image of unity and equality. Larkin focuses particularly on the detail of the clasped hands, presenting the couple as an idealised image of marital fidelity enduring across the centuries: 'faithfulness in effigy'. But the reader should be alert to the double-edged nature of this description, which could mean either that they are the *very* image of fidelity (i.e. the epitome) or that they are *only* the image of fidelity. The blurred and time-eroded monument itself symbolises questionable testimony, as its exact form and the inscription are not entirely clear.

This poem has links to other poems in *The Whitsun Weddings* that deal with marriage and relationships. The deceptive symbolism of the clasped hands recalls the deceptive songbooks in 'Love Songs in Age', which also conceal a deeper and more hurtful lesson about love. The fixedness and hardness of this stony couple recalls the inflexible marital routines represented in 'Afternoons' and 'Self's the Man', and the physical image of the 'supine stationary' couple lying next to each other on the tomb recalls the image of a couple lying side by side in increasingly stony silence in 'Talking in Bed'.

Time

The age of the monument is immediately evident from the eroded and 'blurred' stone, and confirmed by the reference to the 'pre-baroque' in stanza 2. The span of years from past to present now opens for the reader; the clasped hands, like the songbooks in 'Love Songs in Age' and the jazz record in 'Reference Back', provide an intimate link to the past. The use of words such as 'so long', 'prolong', 'early' and 'succeeding' in stanzas 3 and 4 maintains this focus on the issue of time and its passing. The reader is drawn 'through lengths and breadths/Of time', moving backwards and forwards along a thread connecting distant points. The length of time is emphasised by the seasonal repetition of snow, which falls 'undated', summer sunlight and birdsong, and the passing of 'endless altered people'. The past in a sense becomes meaningless as the couple are seen existing still in 'An unarmorial age' to which they do not belong, wallowing in a 'trough/Of smoke in slow suspended skeins/Above their scrap of history'. It is as if their era has been overlaid by successive accretions of time, until all that remains is a deceptive 'attitude' of 'Untruth'. Through this poem Larkin explores the issue of what survives through time and the veracity of lasting monuments, questioning the romantic notion that 'What will survive of us is love'.

Language

Vocabulary of length, breadth and depth

In a poem dealing with love and its impact across time, length, breadth and depth convey a sense of love's power. Such dimensions or lines are not to be understood solely in their physical sense, but also have temporal and spiritual overtones within the poem:

- The phrase 'linked, through lengths and breadths/Of time' demonstrates the endurance of the monument.
- The couple, we are informed, 'would not think to lie so long'.

- Visitors to the church are described as 'endless altered people'; they represent an unbroken link between the past and the present.
- The present is described as 'a trough/Of smoke', suggesting its dislocation from the past; this trough, suggestive of length and depth, hangs 'Above their scrap of history', as if somehow superior to it.

Oxymorons and juxtapositions

Larkin plays with contrasts and uses phrases in which ideas are directly opposed to one another for effect. The sight of the clasped hands of the figures on the monument causes a 'sharp tender shock' — this captures the surprising contrast between the outwardly formal, military nature of the monument and the loving and caring appearance of the couple it commemorates. The monument is described as 'sweet commissioned grace/Thrown off'; the tenderness evoked by 'sweet commissioned' leads us to expect a lovingly crafted monument, but instead it is presented as just another job 'thrown off'. The couple's history after death is described as a 'stationary voyage', an evocative phrase capturing the stillness of the monument, and its ongoing passage through time.

Medieval and archaic vocabulary

The poem deals with the passage of time and uses language designed to evoke a past era of medieval romance and chivalry. Key examples include:

- 'proper' — this is a heraldic term for anything depicted in its natural colour
- 'blazon' — this refers to the description of elements on the heraldic device; it represents a formalised and sanctioned public image
- 'faithfulness in effigy' — this suggests a certain unreality
- 'pre-baroque' — the baroque is a specific architectural and musical period from the late sixteenth to the early eighteenth centuries; it was highly ornamental, in contrast to the austerity of the tomb
- 'tenantry' — one of the orders of medieval society, the tenant farmers of the landowners
- 'jointed armour' — this reference to archaic military apparel creates distance between the reader and the couple; later there is deliberate contrast with the word 'unarmorial'
- 'The Latin names around the base' — this suggests the distant time in which the monument was made

Double meanings

Larkin employs three significant double meanings in the course of the poem:

- 'proper' — this word has the specific heraldic meaning discussed above, but also means clean, correct or mannerly
- 'hardly' — in the phrase 'The stone fidelity/They hardly meant' Larkin exploits this word to mean both 'scarcely' and 'in hard form'

- 'lie' — in the line 'They would not think to lie so long', Larkin points to the supine state of the couple on the monument, but also suggests the underlying deception — the lie of perfect and eternal unity — that the poem turns out to be based upon

Imagery

Erosion

This is an important concept because the poem deals with the passage of time and its impact on perceptions of events. Erosion relates to the nature and endurance of love and the changes time makes to it. The poem is an attempt to re-create the story of the earl and countess by reading their lives and their meaning from the blurred faces and time-eroded monument.

The couple lie with 'their faces blurred', which identifies the influence of time on the stone of the monument and on the view we have of the couple it commemorates. Like their faces, the couple's clothes are changed by the passage of time: 'Their proper habits vaguely shown'. This suggests ill definition, imprecision and fading of colour. The plainness of the monument 'Hardly involves the eye', suggesting an erosion of interest and engagement, and the endless flow of people coming to look at the monument all have their impact on the couple and change their nature, like an eroding sea 'Washing at their identity'.

The observation that 'eyes begin/To look, not read' the Latin inscription sums up the erosion of traditional knowledge. Arguably, the poem 'erodes' the reader's view of love, its meaning and its power to endure.

The dogs

The dogs under the earl and countess's feet are described as a 'faint hint of the absurd', at odds with the formality and seriousness of the rest of the monument and what it represents. They also suggest domesticity, an idea which is compatible with the apparent happiness of the couple. In heraldry, dogs are associated with loyalty, so the presence of the dogs can be seen as a symbol of the couple's supposed fidelity.

Stone

Stone is the material from which the monument is made, but it also has a number of significant figurative connotations. It implies coldness, an idea at odds with the love apparently celebrated in the poem. As the poem progresses, though, and we become increasingly aware of underlying untruth, coldness becomes more appropriate. Stone implies solidity and the unchangeable, but from the outset we learn that the faces of the couple are blurred, demonstrating that even stone is not immutable. As the poem progresses, changes to our view of the couple take place. The reference to 'stone fidelity' is deceptive. It is easy to assume that because something is durable it must be true and faithful, but as the poem shows, this is not necessarily so.

The voyage

In death and in their monumental form, the earl and countess undertake what Larkin refers to as a 'supine stationary voyage'. It is a journey; out of life, through death and into what lies beyond; through time from the 'pre-baroque' past into the present 'unarmorial age'; from deception into what is taken for established truth — 'The stone fidelity/They hardly meant has come to be/Their final blazon'.

Opposites

Public and private

The monument to the earl and countess offers a public view of the private. The 'sharp tender shock' of the clasped hands is a touchingly personal detail in the midst of formality, as is the comic domesticity of the dogs. However, this is the view presented for display — the acceptable version of their relationship. The monument is 'sweet commissioned grace', and as such is not necessarily true. Throughout the poem Larkin hints at the differences that exist between what is publicly shown and what was privately done and felt.

Life and death

In this poem the states of life and death intermingle. The couple lie as if alive on top of the monument to their deaths. The monument lives on into the present, a living record of their death. The ending of the poem questions whether love is more powerful and enduring than death — the final statement of the poem suggests as much, but Larkin's manuscript note places the final power with death. Life and death are juxtaposed in the spring birdsong and the 'Bone-riddled ground' of stanza 5. Death in this poem, as elsewhere in Larkin's work, is an absolute force which nothing truly survives.

Sound and silence

Churches are typically quiet and peaceful places, and Larkin conveys a sense of the respectful silence that visitors preserve while viewing the monument. The couple on the monument are silent; it is the stone that speaks for them and determines how we interpret them and their relationship. In stanza 4 the air turns to 'soundless damage' — a silently destructive force that wears away at the image of the past. Sound, meanwhile, is constructed as a positive force when it appears in the fifth stanza in the form of 'A bright/Litter of birdcalls' — a symbol of life enlivening the 'Bone-riddled ground'.

Permanence and change

The final line of the poem, 'What will survive of us is love', underlines the question of what endures and what does not. Enduring images in the poem are the monument, the dogs and the clasped hands of the earl and countess, but Larkin asks whether anything else survives after death. What remains of this couple is an image of love, 'faithfulness in effigy', but this proves deceptive and hollow, the real 'truth' about them having been blurred.

Truth and deception

The poem seems to be based around the romantic 'truth' of enduring love embodied by the statue on the tomb. However, the reality is much more equivocal: the monument only proves 'Our almost-instinct almost true'. Love remains as 'an attitude', not necessarily as 'truth'. Indeed, Larkin states that 'Time has transfigured them into/Untruth' — the statue is 'The stone fidelity/They hardly meant'. His discovery that their clasped hands were not an original part of the monument adds to the sense that the image of love and truth on which the poem hinges is therefore in itself a deception.

Notes on the other poems

'Nothing to be Said'

This poem considers fundamental issues of life and death, the common denominators of human experience. Regardless of social custom and cultural norms, or one's ethnicity or geographical environment, life is a slow and steady 'advance/On death'. The **zeugma** of 'giving evidence/Or birth' is noteworthy, as is the socially incongruous juxtaposition of 'hunting pig/Or holding a garden-party'. As so often in Larkin, the overriding idea is of a line leading to a central and unavoidable hub: birth is the beginning of death.

'Love Songs in Age'

This is a tender and pathetic poem. It explores the emotions and retrospective views of an old woman/widow thinking over her life. Looking back on her experiences of marriage, a reflection stimulated by a consideration of some sheet music for love songs, she is forced to the painful realisation that romanticised love is an illusion. The real experience falls short of the ideal, as an arrow falls short of its target (compare 'The Whitsun Weddings'.) The poem doubtless reflects on the marriage of Larkin's parents and in particular the experiences of his mother, Eva. Music is often a reminder of disappointment in Larkin's poetry.

'Naturally the Foundation will Bear your Expenses'

This poem re-creates the persona's flight from London to Bombay. It is a sardonic reflection on English culture and the end of Empire. The 'Comet' of stanza 1 is a prototype jet aeroplane. Stanza 2 is a satirical response to the events of Remembrance Day ('solemn-sinister/Wreath-rubbish'). The Morgan Forster referred to in stanza 3 is the novelist Edward Morgan Forster, author of the celebrated novel

A Passage to India. The title is a satirical quotation from an offer of employment; the persona is a name-dropping, jet-setting, socially pretentious literary academic anxious to publish (Chatto is the name of an academic publisher), who has just given the same lecture at Berkeley university in California as he plans to give in Bombay. Auster is the south wind, after which Australia is named.

'Broadcast'

This poem evokes the poet listening to a radio broadcast of a classical music concert. Larkin wrote this poem for Maeve Brennan, one of the women with whom he had a long-term relationship, on the occasion of her attending such a concert. Larkin's dislike of the overtly composed and what he considered soulless nature of this music ('still and withering//Leaves on half-emptied trees'), as compared to the freedom of his beloved jazz, is evident. His affectionate focus on personal details — the gloves, the shoes, the hands — of the woman and his passionate sense of loss in her absence is striking ('Leaving me desperate'). However, he guiltily loses her in the overwhelming sense of the music and thus this is a failed love poem, as he cannot concentrate on his beloved or pick her out in a crowd.

'Faith Healing'

The presentation of the faith healer, an American evangelist, is less than flattering. A domineering and in many ways impressive figure, he is nevertheless exposed as a charlatan and a (dangerous?) fraud. The contrast between the dominant male and his attendant middle-aged, sheep-like females is a key feature of the poem. The final focus on the absence of love and the 'immense slackening ache' this creates — an ache beyond the powers of the healer ('That nothing cures') — provides the pathetic conclusion and leaves the impression of lives led in emptiness and deception.

'For Sidney Bechet'

Sidney Bechet (1897–1959) was a celebrated jazz saxophonist. Living and working in New Orleans with fellow jazz pioneers such as Louis Armstrong, he was one of the most influential musicians in the creation and development of jazz music. The poem demonstrates Larkin's love for jazz and evocatively creates the atmosphere of Storyville (a famous jazz club in New Orleans) and the French Quarter of the city. The entire city seems to be summed up in Bechet's playing ('That note you hold, narrowing and rising, shakes/Like New Orleans reflected on the water') and is described as 'the natural noise of good'. This is an entirely and rarely affirmative poem, 'an enormous yes'.

'Home is so Sad'

This is an elegiac and deeply wistful poem. Home is personified and imagined in the absence of its 'owners'. The poem considers the way humans shape their environment to their needs and personalities. 'A joyous shot at how things ought to be,/Long fallen wide' is a recurring and central image in Larkin's work — the arrow which misses its target, the hope which is never realised.

'Toads Revisited'

This is a poem about work and its significance. As the title implies, it follows on from a poem entitled 'Toads', published in Larkin's earlier collection *The Less Deceived*. For all its frustrations and negatives, the 'toad work' is seen as preferable to idleness, since routine staves off absence. Work offers fulfilment where the empty pastimes and bleak lives encountered in the park do not. As so often, Larkin recognises a common predicament with those he despises; in this case it is that they are all travelling down Cemetery Road, again an image of a line leading to a terminus.

'Water'

This is a poem about religion and religious belief. The central image of water is significant in Christianity (baptism, source of life, rivers etc.). The poem encourages thoughts of change ('a fording/To dry, different clothes') and makes use of muscular vocabulary (e.g. 'sousing', 'furious devout drench'). Light, with which the poem ends, is also a significant image within the Christian tradition. The combination of water and light, as in the rainbow, is a radiant transfiguration of ordinariness into the transcendental.

'Self's the Man'

The persona of the poem, a single man, weighs up the pros and cons of singleness and marriage. The tone of the poem is satirical and at times harsh, as the apparently unselfish act of sharing one's life with a wife and children is seen to be just as selfishly motivated as remaining single. The poem presents a jaded view of marriage, though the title and expression are jocular as well as colloquial, and the rhyming couplets create a comic effect. The italics represent the voice of Arnold's wife, who is being mocked.

'Take One Home for the Kiddies'

The title of the poem calls attention to the invasiveness of advertising and consumerism in 1960s Britain. The scenario of children nagging their mother for a pet (evidently kept in poor conditions in the pet shop) is familiar. The animals are soon forgotten, however, and die ('Fetch the shoebox, fetch the shovel'). The emotionless and northern voices of the children, in italics, are bleakly funny, contrasting with the pathos of the animals' brief lives. The brevity of the animals' lives, and the children's interest, is reflected in the short repeated structure of the poem. However, the change of metre between the first and second stanza from iambic to trochaic moves the mood from tragic to comic.

'Days'

This short poem illustrates the repetitiveness and futility of life, days being a time and place. The routine and resigned tone of the poem lead only to an acceptance of the inevitability of death, when the last rites are performed by the priest, and the death certificate is signed by the doctor.

'MCMXIV'

Set at the beginning of the First World War, this is a poignant and elegiac poem that seems to be scrutinising a photograph. The lines of men queuing to enlist for the army are blissfully unaware of the horrors they are to experience in the trenches, which will not be a game. The poem's wistful tone celebrates innocence and a bygone age very different from either the postwar 1950s or the decadent 1960s. The inevitability of death and irrevocable change hangs over the verse, which is restrained and elegant. The Roman numerals for 1914 are suggestive of a tombstone or archaic document, and are redolent of history. There are many references to details of the domestic and social life of the period, and the security of knowing one's class and place. Because of the use of semi-colons the whole poem is technically one sentence. The flow of life from William the Conqueror was interrupted for ever by the Great War, which irrecoverably turned innocence into experience.

'Talking in Bed'

The title of this poem leads the reader to expect intimacy and love. However, the conditional tense 'ought to' in the opening line suggests a different reality. As words fail within this relationship, honesty and kindness are ever harder to attain and are swapped for concealment and silence. The threatening 'dark towns' of stanza 3 point to troubles in the relationship, which is growingly characterised by 'isolation'. The repeated double negative of the final line emphasises the paradox of the close/distant relationship, and of the fact that the best humans can do for each other is not to lie or be cruel: truth and kindness are out of the question.

'The Large Cool Store'

The new consumer culture of the 1960s, with its fashions and bright colours, is the focus here. The store is a world of variety and choice. However, Larkin is alert to the realities of production and the 'weekday world of those//Who leave at dawn' to make all these goods. He points to the false and deceptive promises of the marketing men who convince the consumer that 'their sort is/Matched by' the clothes on offer and that the purchaser can buy into an identity. The use of 'unreal', 'synthetic' and 'natureless' in the final stanza illustrates the ultimately hollow nature of consumerism and the promises on which it is based. The alternate rhyme scheme draws attention to two contrasting states and perceptions: work and play; natural and artificial; dull and bright.

'A Study of Reading Habits'

The persona reflects on his range of reading as a child, when he was full of enthusiasm for books, and as a young adult, when horror and pornography seem to have been his choice. In later life, however, tired of formulaic fiction, he prefers to take refuge in drink and abandons reading, having learned that what happens in books is only a fantasy, and that in real life people are not brave, 'cool' and heroic, but disappointing, cowardly and dull.

'As Bad as a Mile'

The title recalls the saying 'A miss is as bad as a mile'. The poem traces in reverse a failed attempt to throw an apple core into a waste bin, which is symbolic of a failed life. The final image of the uneaten apple embodies all the potential that has gone to waste, or rather the temptation that was not succumbed to, and therefore the lack of living. As in many other Larkin poems, including 'The Whitsun Weddings', the image is one of a trajectory towards a target.

'Ambulances'

The threatening ambulances seem to prowl the streets of the city, the focus of attention of all they pass. They are a ubiquitous presence ('All streets in time are visited'), symbolising sickness and functioning as a *memento mori*. They create fear in those who see them and those who enter them ('A wild white face'), pointing to 'the solving emptiness/That lies just under all we do', i.e. death. The long flowing sentences Larkin employs reflect the fluid, almost ghostly movement of the ambulances through the streets, threads that all lead to the hospital.

'The Importance of Elsewhere'

Larkin moved to Belfast in 1950, where he worked as a sub-librarian at Queen's University. In this poem he explores the emotions evoked by moving over the sea to a 'foreign' place, an experience dislocating but also strangely safe, free from censure and the constraints of 'customs and establishments'. He identifies the indulgence afforded to the outsider, which provides a kind of security — the word 'underwrites' invokes the idea of insurance — not available to him in England, his native land. Larkin's use of slightly discordant rhyme throughout the poem may reflect its concern with difference.

'Sunny Prestatyn'

This is a disturbingly violent, even misogynistic poem. The poster of a girl in swimwear suggestive of bridal wear and virginity, who is advertising Prestatyn (a Welsh seaside resort), has been defaced in a brutal and sexually explicit way in a poem containing many references to male and female body parts. The change of language register in the second stanza is shocking. The final lines of the poem seem almost dismissive of what has happened. This reflects, perhaps, on Larkin's own views as an avid collector of pornography. The power of advertising to provoke violence in the socially deprived is made clear by showing how it teasingly presents desirable but unobtainable objects which are 'too good for this life', and how it trades on deception: Prestatyn is not always sunny, nor full of attractive women. Its exaggerated claims make it possible to sympathise with, or at least understand, Titch Thomas, who refuses to be deceived by the whore of advertising. Cancer is a fact belonging to grimmer reality.

'First Sight'

This poem emphasises the fragility of life, as the newborn lambs face 'a vast unwelcome'. The use of the adjective as a noun here is striking and drives home the vulnerability of the creatures in the threatening winter — 'a wretched width of cold'. The harshness of winter existence, however, does not last forever, as Larkin points out. 'Earth's immeasurable surprise', the coming spring, lies just around the corner with its promise of life. The fourth line of the second stanza is metrically irregular to convey the miracle of the waking earth. Lambs have traditionally been used in literature to represent innocence, but also vulnerability. One cannot help thinking of other, less pleasant, surprises in store for the lambs.

'Ignorance'

Uncertainties and 'imprecisions' are the focus of this poem. The equivocations of stanza 1 ('*or so I feel, /*Or *Well, it does seem so*') set the scene. Larkin's repeated use of the word 'strange', which occurs three times, emphasises his reaction to such prevarication and the ignorance it suggests. He points to the certainty of life ('our flesh/Surrounds us with its own decisions') and the inevitability of death ('when we start to die'). Seed is used elsewhere in Larkin's work as an image of an end contained in a beginning, death within life, started by the gesture of spreading/broadcasting in lines from a central point, like a railway journey.

Reference Back

Larkin's love of jazz emerges in this poem. The Oliver referred to in stanza 2 is Joe 'King' Oliver, a legendary jazz artist and leader of the Creole Jazz Band. *Riverside Blues* is one of their famous numbers. The poem deals with the relationship between a son and his mother and begins with their differing responses to the music, which reveal the generation gap. The mother's response evidently annoys the son and the repeated use of 'unsatisfactory' makes clear his dislike of being at home, which contrasts with the mother's love of these visits. The music provides a 'sudden bridge' — note the musical pun on the word 'bridge' (the section of music between verse and chorus) — which brings home to the son how much he has lost and what opportunities he has missed. The music, in its freedom and vivacity, accentuates the limitations of his existence at home. As in 'Dockery and Son', the persona laments the fact that time makes choices for us without our being aware of them until too late.

'Wild Oats'

The persona here (Andrew Motion links this persona to Larkin himself when working in Wellington) explores his contrasting relationships with two girls, one 'bosomy' and attractive who he has not the bravery to address, and the other, 'in specs', less attractive but more approachable. The poem takes a cynical view of romance, evident in the price of the ring and the emphasis on numbers generally. After all the love letters, the ring and the trysts, he is told that he is 'too selfish, withdrawn,/And easily bored to love'. Photographs are a recurring motif in Larkin's work, as a tangible form of a lost past, an opportunity not taken or an idealised unobtainable vision of something too good for this life. The title refers to the belief that young men need to sew their wild oats, i.e. to have sexual experience before settling into marriage, so it is being used ironically in that the relationship was not sexual, or wild in any sense, and in that these particular seeds, i.e. the relationship, had no potential for growth. Note the word 'shooting-match' to represent sexual desire, arrows being a recurring image in Larkin for fertility and aiming into the future.

'Essential Beauty'

This is another poem dealing with consumer culture. Larkin addresses the issue of advertising and marketing, pointing out in satirical terms the ploys and deceptions used to convince credulous potential purchasers. The concrete and detailed descriptions are, as so often, transcended in the final lines by a reference to light and water, and an image of perfect beauty which, like the pastoral myth depicted in the poem, can never become reality. The dying smokers, conned by advertising into pursuing a fatal illusion, recall the 'Fight Cancer' ending of 'Sunny Prestatyn'.

'Send No Money'

Truth is the focus in this poem (compare 'Essential Beauty', 'Talking in Bed', 'Ignorance'). Searching for the meaning of life, the persona of the poem addresses the grotesque figure of Time ('fobbed/Impendent belly'). Ultimately, however, it is only the battering of experience, 'what happened to happen', that can show 'the way things go'. The final evaluation of truth as a 'trite untransferable/Truss-advertisement' sums up his view, in disgust expressed by the explosive 't' alliteration, that advertising, which by definition tells lies while claiming to proclaim truth, has debased and devalued the very concept. The poem's title comes from an advertising cliché designed to lure the unsuspecting consumer.

'Afternoons'

This is another poem dealing with marriage and children (compare 'Dockery and Son', 'Self's the Man', 'An Arundel Tomb', 'The Whitsun Weddings' and 'Talking in Bed'). The initial line — 'Summer is fading' — suggests a coming change, a movement towards harsh winter; autumn is the traditional elegiac season. The working class characters of this poem find themselves marginalised within their own lives by the demands of marriage and children. The photo album records an idealised romantic past which has since become diminished by everyday routines. Unripe acorns are the seeds of the future; like the seasons, the generations succeed each other relentlessly and ruthlessly.

Extracts from *Jill* and *A Girl in Winter*

These extracts from Larkin's two early novels are notable for their similarities with his later poetry. Capturing the essence of a moment, telling descriptive details and the subtle but pervasive use of opposites — traits which characterise these passages — are typical of the poems in *The Whitsun Weddings*. In the extracts Larkin displays an evident love of the natural world and an ability to convey essential beauty, which are tempered by an aura of melancholy and a fascination with human suffering.

Extract 1: *Jill* (1946)

John Kemp sat in the corner of an empty compartment in a train travelling over the last stretch of line before Oxford. It was nearly four o'clock on a Thursday in the middle of October, and the air had begun to thicken as it always does before a dusk in autumn. The sky had become stiff with opaque clouds. When they were clear of the gasometers, the wagons and blackened bridges of Banbury, he looked out over the fields, noticing the clumps of trees that sped by, whose dying leaves each had an individual colour, from palest ochre to nearly purple, so that each tree stood out distinctly as in spring. The hedges were still green, but the leaves of the convolvuli threaded through them had turned sickly yellow, and from a distance looked like late flowers. Little arms of rivers twisted through the meadows, lined with willows that littered the surface with leaves. The waters were spanned by empty foot-bridges.

It looked cold and deserted. The windows of the carriages were bluish with the swirls of the cleaner's leather still showing on the glass, and he confined his eyes to the compartment. It was a third-class carriage, and the crimson seats smelt of dust and engines and tobacco, but the air was warm. Pictures of Dartmouth Castle and Portmadoc looked at him from the opposite wall. He was an undersized boy, eighteen years old, with a pale face and soft pale hair brushed childishly from left to right. Lying back against the seat, he stretched his legs out and pushed his hands to the bottom of the pockets of his cheap blue overcoat. The lapels of it curled outwards and creases dragged from the buttons. His face was thin, and perhaps strained; the expression round his mouth was ready to become taut, and a small frown lingered on his forehead. His whole appearance lacked luxuriance. Only his silky hair, as soft as seeding thistle, gave him an air of beauty.

Extract 2: *A Girl in Winter*

There had been no more snow during the night, but because the frost continued so that the drifts lay where they had fallen, people told each other there was more to come. And when it grew lighter, it seemed that they were right, for there was no sun, only one vast shell of cloud over the fields and woods. In contrast to the snow the sky looked brown. Indeed, without the snow the morning would have resembled a January nightfall, for what light there was seemed to rise up from it.

It lay in ditches and in hollows in the fields, where only birds walked. In some lanes the wind had swept it up faultlessly to the very tops of the hedges. Villages were cut off until gangs of men could clear a passage on the roads; the labourers could not go out to work, and on the aerodromes near these villages all flying remained cancelled. People who lay ill in bed could see the shine off the ceilings of their rooms, and a puppy confronted with it for the first time howled and crept under the water-butt. The out-houses were roughly powdered down the windward side, the fences were half-submerged like breakwaters; the whole landscape was so white and still it might have been a formal painting. People were unwilling to get up. To look at the snow too long had a hypnotic effect, drawing away all power of concentration, and the cold seemed to cramp the bones, making work harder and unpleasant. Nevertheless, the candles had to be lit, and the ice in the jugs smashed, and the milk unfrozen; the men had to be given their breakfasts and got off to work in the yards. Life had to be carried on, in no matter what circumscribed way; even though one went no further than the window-seat, there was plenty to be done indoors, saved for such time as this.

But through cuttings and along embankments ran the railway lines, and although they were empty, they led on northwards and southwards till they began to join, passing factories that had worked all night, and the backs of houses where light showed round the curtains, reaching the cities where the snow was disregarded, and which the frost could only besiege for a few days, bitterly.

Quotations

Larkin's views

Larkin's view of himself

To me I seem very much an outsider, yet I suppose 99% of people would say I'm very much establishment and conventional. Funny isn't it?.

(quoted in *Philip Larkin: A Writer's Life,* Motion, 1993)

Children

Children are often bored, I think. They don't control their destinies, and they don't do what they want or live where they want.

(*South Bank Show* interview with Melvyn Bragg, 1981)

Until I began to meet grown-ups on more or less equal terms I fancied myself a kind of Ishmael. The realisation that it was not people I disliked but children was for me one of those celebrated moments of revelation.

('The Savage Seventh' in *Required Writings*, 1983)

Marriage

It would be somewhat absurd of me to regret [my father's] marriage, but I could never see why he needed a wife. He liked his own company best and gloried in his ability to look after himself, and his clumsiness in human relations must have made him an unsatisfactory husband, which in turn must have put a certain strain on him. Certainly the marriage left me with two convictions: that human beings should not live together, and that children should be taken from their parents at an early age.

(The Philip Larkin Archive, Brynmor Jones Library, Notebook 5)

Poetry

People say I'm very negative, and I suppose I am, but the impulse for producing a poem is never negative; the most negative poem in the world is a very positive thing to have done.

(The Philip Larkin Archive, Brynmor Jones Library, Notebook 4)

It is sometimes useful to remind ourselves of the simpler aspects of things normally regarded as complicated. Take, for instance, the writing of a poem. It consists of three stages: the first is when a man becomes obsessed with an emotional concept to such a degree that he is compelled to do something about it. What he does is the second stage, namely, construct a verbal device that will reproduce this emotional concept in anyone who cares to read it, anywhere, any time. The third stage is the recurrent situation of people in different times and places setting off the device and re-creating in themselves what the poet felt when he wrote it. The stages are interdependent and all necessary. If there has been no preliminary feeling, the device has nothing to reproduce and the reader will experience nothing. If the second stage has not been well done, the device will not deliver the goods, or will deliver only a few goods to a few people, or will stop delivering them after an absurdly short while. And if there is no third stage, no successful reading, the poem can hardly be said to exist at all.

What a description of this basic structure shows is that poetry is emotional in nature and theatrical in operation, a skilled re-creation of emotion in other people, and that a bad poem is one that never succeeds in doing this. All modes of criticism are no more than different ways of saying this, whatever literary, philosophical or moral terminology they employ, and it would not be necessary to point out anything so obvious if present-day poetry did not suggest that it had been forgotten. ('The Pleasure Principle' in *Required Writings*, 1983)

It is not sufficient to say that poetry has lost its audience, and so need no longer consider it: lots of people still read and even buy poetry. More accurately, poetry has lost its old audience, and gained a new one. This has been caused by the consequences of a cunning merger between poet, literary critic and academic critic (three classes now notoriously indistinguishable): it is hardly an exaggeration to say that the poet has gained the happy position wherein he can praise his own poetry in the press and explain it in the classroom; the reader has been bullied into giving up the consumer's power to say 'I don't like this, bring me something different.'
('The Pleasure Principle' in *Required Writings*, 1983)

Art

What I don't believe about art is that it should require special knowledge or special training on the part of its consumers. Art is enjoyment, first on the part of the writer, painter or musician, and then, by communication, on the part of the reader and looker and listener. (letter to Steve Race)

Jazz

There are not many perfect things in jazz, but [Sidney] Bechet playing the blues could be one of them... ('A Real Musicianer', *Guardian*, 8 April 1960)

Jazz is to be appreciated not as a musical exercise in technique, but as an emotional experience, one that can exhilarate or sadden.
(address to students at Hull University, *Torchlight 69*, 23 October 1962)

I can live a week without poetry but not a day without jazz.
('Poet on the 8.15', interview with J. Hodder, *Guardian*, 20 May 1965)

From the poems

It is important to learn some useful quotations and think about how you would use them. Make notes on how you could use each of these quotations to support your views on Larkin's poetry.

A cut-price crowd, urban yet simple — 'Here'

Loneliness clarifies. — ibid.

Here is unfenced existence:
Facing the sun, untalkative, out of reach. — ibid.

how we live measures our own nature — 'Mr Bleaney'

Life is slow dying. — 'Nothing to be Said'

the unfailing sense of being young
Spread out like a spring-woken tree — 'Love Songs in Age'

Crowds, colourless and caveworn — 'Naturally the Foundation will Bear your Expenses'

I think of your face among all those faces — 'Broadcast'

In everyone there sleeps
A sense of life lived according to love — 'Faith Healing'

A joyous shot at how things ought to be — 'Home is so Sad'

Give me your arm, old toad;
Help me down Cemetery Road. — 'Toads Revisited'

As if out on the end of an event
Waving goodbye
To something that survived it. — 'The Whitsun Weddings'

this frail
Travelling coincidence — ibid.

each face seemed to define
Just what it saw departing ibid.

there swelled
A sense of falling, like an arrow-shower
Sent out of sight, somewhere becoming rain. — ibid.

But wait, not so fast:
Is there such a contrast? — 'Self's the Man'

What are days for?	'Days'
Never such innocence again.	'MCMXIV'
An emblem of two people being honest.	'Talking in Bed
It becomes still more difficult to find Words at once true and kind, Or not untrue and not unkind.	ibid.
How separate and unearthly love is	'The Large Cool Store'
The women I clubbed with sex!	'A Study of Reading Habits'
Books are a load of crap.	ibid.
the solving emptiness That lies just under all we do	'Ambulances'
Brings closer what is left to come, And dulls to distance all we are.	ibid.
Strangeness made sense.	'The Importance of Elsewhere'
Here no elsewhere underwrites my existence.	ibid.
She was slapped up one day in March.	'Sunny Prestatyn'
She was too good for this life.	ibid.
Earth's immeasurable surprise.	'First Sight'
the ranged Joining and parting lines reflect a strong Unhindered moon.	'Dockery and Son'
the shock Of finding out how much had gone of life, How widely from the others	ibid.
Life is first boredom, then fear.	ibid.
And leaves what something hidden from us chose, And age, and then the only end of age.	ibid.
Strange to know nothing, never to be sure Of what is true or right or real	'Ignorance'
We are not suited to the long perspectives Open at each instant of our lives. They link us to our losses	'Reference Back'

I was too selfish, withdrawn,
And easily bored to love. — 'Wild Oats'

sharply-pictured groves
Of how life should be. — 'Essential Beauty'

Tracing the trite untransferable
Truss-advertisement, truth. — 'Send No Money'

Something is pushing them
To the side of their own lives. — 'Afternoons'

One sees, with a sharp tender shock,
His hand withdrawn, holding her hand. — 'An Arundel Tomb'

They would not think to lie so long. — ibid.

Time has transfigured them into
Untruth. — ibid.

Literary terms and concepts

Assessment Objective 1 requires 'insight appropriate to literary study, using appropriate terminology'. The terms below are relevant to *The Whitsun Weddings* and will aid concise argument and expression.

alliteration — repetition of initial letter or sound in adjacent words, e.g. 'silence stand' ('Here')

allusion — reference, either direct or indirect, to another text, e.g. 'Oliver's *Riverside Blues*' ('Reference Back')

antithesis — contrast of ideas expressed by setting them against one another

assonance — repetition of vowel sounds in words of close proximity, e.g. 'faint/Archaic' ('The Importance of Elsewhere')

bathos — descent from the elevated to the commonplace

black humour — humour that makes fun of something serious or sad

caesura — deliberate break or pause in a line of poetry, signified by punctuation

cliché — predictable and overused expression or situation, e.g. 'As Bad as a Mile'

colloquialism informal language of conversational speech, e.g. 'It used to make me throw up' ('Naturally the Foundation will Bear your Expenses')

conceit clever thought conveyed by a surprising image or an extended figure of speech

connotations implications of words and phrases that are over and above their obvious meaning

contextuality historical, cultural, social, economic and political background of a text

couplet pair of consecutive rhyming lines

double entendre expression with two meanings, one of them coarse

ellipsis omission of word(s) for economy or avoidance of repetition

enjamb(e)ment run-on line of poetry, usually to reflect its meaning

end-stopped line that is 'stopped' at the end by a punctuation mark

epiphany sudden and striking revelation of the essence of something sublime

feminine ending a light or unstressed syllable at the end of a line of verse, e.g. 'Here no elsewhere underwrites my existence' ('The Importance of Elsewhere')

hyperbole deliberate exaggeration for literary effect

imagery descriptive language appealing to the senses: touch, taste, smell, sight, hearing; often creates pictorial or visual effects, e.g. 'arrow-shower' ('The Whitsun Weddings')

internal rhyme rhyme occurring within a line of poetry

irony language intended to mean the opposite of the words expressed; amusing or cruel reversal of an outcome expected, intended or deserved; situation in which one is mocked by fate or the facts

juxtaposition placing ideas, characters, events etc. side by side for (often ironic) contrast or to create other types of literary connection

litotes understatement for rhetorical effect, especially expressing an affirmative by the negative of its contrary, e.g. 'not bad' for 'good'

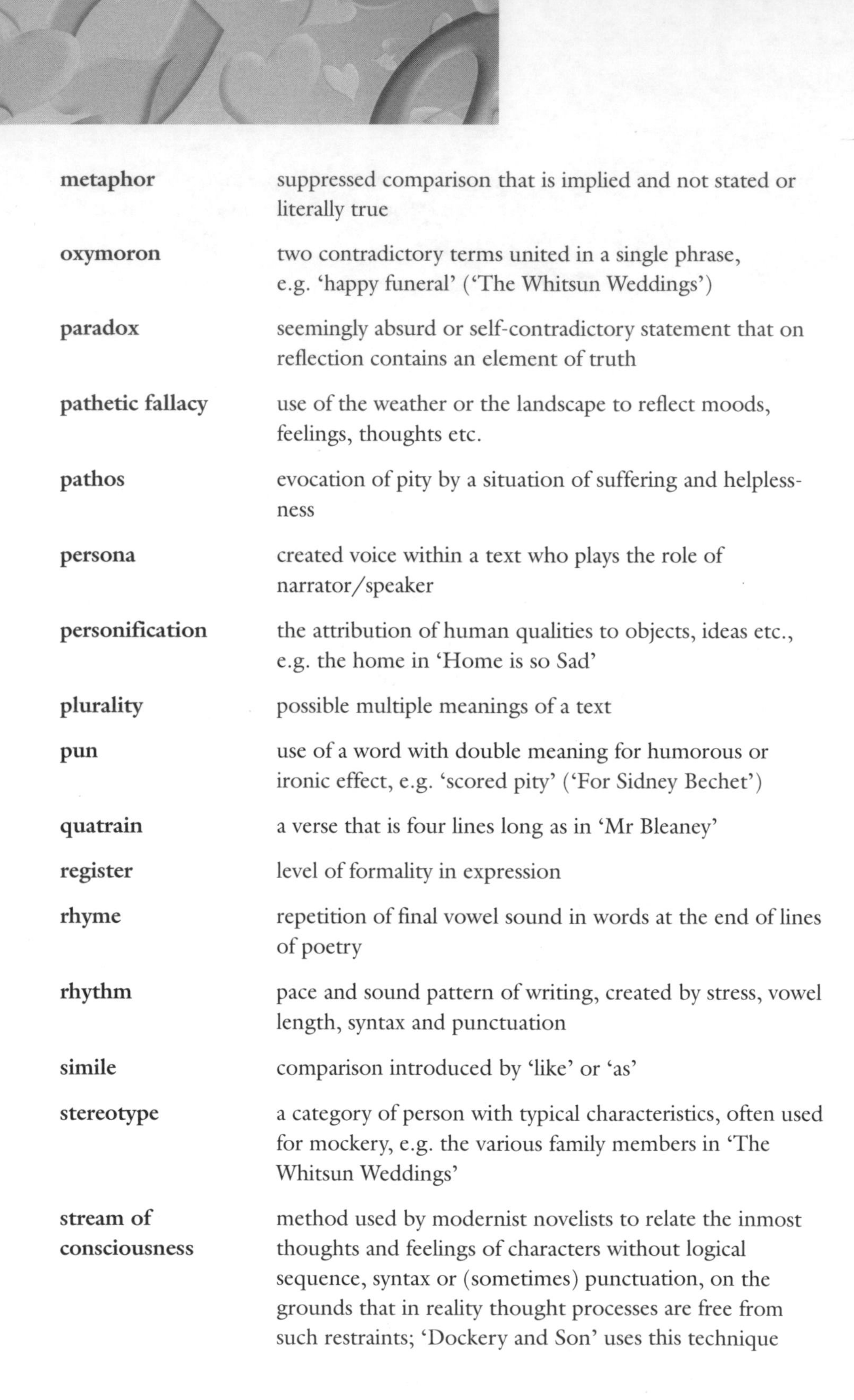

metaphor suppressed comparison that is implied and not stated or literally true

oxymoron two contradictory terms united in a single phrase, e.g. 'happy funeral' ('The Whitsun Weddings')

paradox seemingly absurd or self-contradictory statement that on reflection contains an element of truth

pathetic fallacy use of the weather or the landscape to reflect moods, feelings, thoughts etc.

pathos evocation of pity by a situation of suffering and helplessness

persona created voice within a text who plays the role of narrator/speaker

personification the attribution of human qualities to objects, ideas etc., e.g. the home in 'Home is so Sad'

plurality possible multiple meanings of a text

pun use of a word with double meaning for humorous or ironic effect, e.g. 'scored pity' ('For Sidney Bechet')

quatrain a verse that is four lines long as in 'Mr Bleaney'

register level of formality in expression

rhyme repetition of final vowel sound in words at the end of lines of poetry

rhythm pace and sound pattern of writing, created by stress, vowel length, syntax and punctuation

simile comparison introduced by 'like' or 'as'

stereotype a category of person with typical characteristics, often used for mockery, e.g. the various family members in 'The Whitsun Weddings'

stream of consciousness method used by modernist novelists to relate the inmost thoughts and feelings of characters without logical sequence, syntax or (sometimes) punctuation, on the grounds that in reality thought processes are free from such restraints; 'Dockery and Son' uses this technique

synecdoche	form of metaphor in which a part (often a body part) is used to represent the whole
theme	abstract idea or issue explored in a text
tone	emotional aspect of the voice of a text
zeugma	yoking together of two incongruous nouns through their shared grammatical structure, e.g. 'Hours giving evidence/Or birth' ('Nothing to be Said')

Student Text Guide

Questions & Answers

LITERATURE

The Whitsun Weddings

Essay questions, specimen plans and notes

The exemplar essay questions which follow can be used for planning practice and/or full essay writing within the time limit, with or without the text. Possible plans are given to show how the titles may be approached. These are suggested responses only and other approaches may be equally valid. Of course, the points identified would need to be illustrated with well-chosen examples and quotations from the text. Accompanying each plan are examiner comments specific to the tasks, which illustrate how the Assessment Objectives are applied by examiners.

Remember to talk about the poem and the persona, not the poet, and try to hear how the poem would sound if read aloud. Form and language are essential elements of poetry, so you must not restrict yourself to a discussion of content. Where appropriate, you may choose to incorporate relevant critical material as a basis for your argument and response.

The question you choose may direct you to one or two prescribed poems or ask you to select your own. Either way you should think about the following:

- Careful selection of poems is crucial to ensure the relevance and success of your essay. The poems you like or are most familiar with are not necessarily the most appropriate for a particular title.
- Show your knowledge of the whole selection as well as your response to and analysis of particular poems.
- Focus closely on the chosen poem(s) but also relate their content and/or language to elsewhere in the selection. Examiners advise that a substantial portion (up to 60%) of responses to passage-based questions should refer to the rest of the work being studied. Link your comments to the overall themes, and suggest ways in which the poem is typical of the poet's work as a whole.
- Don't waste time paraphrasing what happens in a poem; just give a quick summary of its setting and context, noting who is present, where and why.
- Think about reader reaction, using your own as the basis for your response.
- For an open-book exam you will have made annotations in the margin and on the text, but only include the relevant ones, and remember that they need to be organised into a structured response, not just transferred to your essay as a list.

Questions and plans

1 'Larkin is often thought of as a gloomy poet, describing the world around him in a drab and depressing way. Yet this is only half of Larkin.' Explore this idea, using the poem 'The Whitsun Weddings' as a starting point and examining AT LEAST TWO other poems.

Possible ideas to include in a plan

- Written in the late 1950s and early 1960s, *The Whitsun Weddings* deals with a period of profound social change. The drabness and depression of the postwar years were being replaced by the colour, vibrancy and experimentalism of the 1960s. Larkin's poetry addresses this social awakening.
- Challenge the view that Larkin is always drab and gloomy; point to the use of bright colour and celebration (however ironically it is presented) in 'The Whitsun Weddings' as evidence that there is another side.
- Note the warmth and comfort the traveller feels on the journey to London and the arguably affectionate presentation of weddings. However, also comment on Larkin's views on marriage and the ambiguous nature of the celebrations he describes.
- Consider the final images of the poem and whether they present a positive or a negative view of where these marriages are headed.
- Compare 'The Whitsun Weddings' to 'Dockery and Son', in which there is more unrelieved gloom, with negative views of life, death and the begetting of children. Comment on the use both poems make of the metaphor of railways for life and its events.
- Compare 'The Whitsun Weddings' to 'An Arundel Tomb'. Consider the presentation of the couple and their marriage. Draw out thematic parallels and Larkin's lively picture of the tomb and the earl and the countess. Emphasise the poems' ambivalent celebration and questioning of love and marriage.
- Compare 'The Whitsun Weddings' to 'Mr Bleaney'. Even the depressing picture of bedsit life Larkin draws in the latter is not unrelieved, as he humorously and ironically presents the dreariness of Mr Bleaney's existence.
- Discuss the use of well-observed detail in all of these poems to convey humanity and to 'colour' even the drabbest of pictures.

Examiner's comments

AO1 The standard view of Larkin is described in terms that should not cause problems – gloomy, drab, depressing; the quotation leaves the other half of Larkin undefined. Higher-band answers will respond quickly to this and fill the gap; lower-band answers will see the gloom, but will find it difficult to see the humanity.

AO2 The quotation does not suggest that Larkin wrote straightforwardly 'happy' poems – rather that the misery is not unrelenting; therefore choice of poem is not as significant as what the answer manages to do with it. Nevertheless higher-band answers will select wisely, to make interesting comparisons between poems, discovering different genres – satire, parody, the philosophical. Lower-band answers will not see the variety in the collection and will miss the subtle variations in voice.

AO3 Higher-band answers will address Larkin's imagery – the arrow-shower in 'The Whitsun Weddings', for example – and will note how Larkin's selection of language is significant in portraying 'the other half' of Larkin. Lower-band answers are likely to be limited in their exploration of structure in particular; higher-band answers will see structural features such as the movement from the concrete to the abstract, from (gloomy) industrial shadows to (hopeful?) unfenced existence.

AO4 Answers do not, of course, have to agree with the quotation. However, to be successful they should not dismiss the idea out of hand but may perhaps argue instead that Larkin's humour or hopefulness reflects only a sad acceptance of grim realities. Better answers will be aware that the author is not necessarily the voice of the poem and higher-band answers will recognise the ambiguities in Larkin's poetry. Lower-band answers will probably find it difficult to move beyond the drab and depressing except by inappropriately and excessively used quotation from Larkin's other writings, thereby confusing the man and his poems.

AO5 The phrase 'the world around him' supplies plenty of context here. Higher-band answers will take up the challenge of the question – that the gloomy poet is only half the story. The starting-point poem provides an opportunity for answers to see the hopeful side, especially in its closing imagery. Lower-band answers may find it difficult to move beyond the drab and depressing literal picture and may miss the subtleties, humour, ironies and imagery in Larkin's presentation of the contemporary world.

2 'Poetry has been described as "a fresh look and a fresh listen". Larkin's work fits this description: it challenges what society normally takes for granted.' Examine AT LEAST THREE poems in *The Whitsun Weddings* in the light of this claim.

Possible ideas to include in a plan

- Straddling the postwar years and the newly liberal 1960s, *The Whitsun Weddings* reflects a significant shift in social norms.
- The collection challenges a plethora of clichés (he even uses these as titles), and especially debunks the premise that marriage and children are the purpose of existence.
- Larkin often approaches issues of everyday experience and offers the reader insight into these and new perspectives on them, e.g. marriage in 'The Whitsun Weddings', work in 'Toads Revisited', advertising and commercialism in 'Essential Beauty'.
- In 'The Whitsun Weddings' Larkin takes the reader beyond the simple surface celebration of marriage to look at the ambiguities and long-term implications of the wedding day. He sees the feast and the honeymoon as a microcosm of the meaning of marriage. He explores these issues more fully and critically in poems such as 'Afternoons' and 'Talking in Bed'.
- In 'Toads Revisited' Larkin looks closely at the complex relationship between the individual and work, seeing in the latter's routine and almost mindless repetition a curiously comforting and necessary 'companion', embodied in the ambiguous image of the toad.
- In 'Essential Beauty' Larkin forces the reader to unpick the meanings that lie behind the surface of the advertising world. He lays bare its deceptions, cynicism and attempts to manipulate the consumer.

- In all these poems the poet moves beyond the mundane and the obvious to a more profound view of what these things mean and how they influence the individual.

Examiner's comments

AO1 Candidates are offered Robert Frost's definition of poetry. Despite the slight quaintness of the phrase the basic meaning should not pose a problem to any candidates; it is the sensitivity and thoughtfulness of the interpretation that will distinguish higher- from lower-band answers. A literal reading of 'listen' is unlikely to prove productive, though the poem 'Broadcast' might be used by some here; higher-band answers will take on board the word 'challenge', which is what the question is all about.

AO2 The 'challenging poem' is the genre to be explored here, though higher-band candidates may well find such a definition inadequate for the subtlety and range of Larkin's poetry. Choice of poem might not in itself be a discriminator – all Larkin's poems have the freshness described in the quotation – but the use made of the poems will be; lower-band answers will focus mainly on the reader as someone grappling with meaning rather than someone being challenged.

AO3 Higher-band answers will be aware of how the poetry is structured to allow movement within poems, as perspectives shift and voices change. They may see that Larkin's challenge is often quiet and understated, as his choice of diction shows, but nonetheless powerful. Lower-band answers will not pay much attention to detail of language and form; if quotation is used it is unlikely to be fully exploited.

AO4 Some answers may find Larkin's poetry more conservative than radical and take issue with the quotation. Interpretations that are well supported and relevant are of course welcomed. The discriminator will be the quality of argument and sensitivity to the poetry: higher-band answers will recognise that, conservative though he may be, Larkin is an uneasy and disquieting read; lower-band answers will not appreciate that there is much to discuss here and will possibly remain focused on society and subject matter rather than Larkin's handling of them in his poetry.

AO5 Higher-band answers will appreciate Larkin as a controversialist: rather than merely describing contemporary society or looking back on some golden age, he is offering real social criticism and comment. Lower-band answers are less likely to see the extent to which Larkin is controversial or to link this with the 'fresh look and a fresh listen' quotation.

Further questions

1 Read 'The Whitsun Weddings', paying particular attention to subject matter and style. In what ways do the concerns and stylistic features of this poem reflect those in *The Whitsun Weddings* as a whole?

2 Discuss Larkin's evocation of place in *The Whitsun Weddings* and assess its significance.

3 Larkin's poetry has been criticised for its excessively pessimistic nature. To what extent is this a satisfactory summary of *The Whitsun Weddings*?

4 Remind yourself of the poem 'The Whitsun Weddings'. To what extent do you agree with the view that, in terms of subject matter and style, this poem is the key to the whole collection?

5 Larkin wrote: 'I like to read about people who aren't beautiful or lucky, presented with a realistic firmness and humour.' How far do you feel that *The Whitsun Weddings* presents people like this? In your answer you should EITHER refer to TWO or THREE poems OR range more widely through the collection.

6 Remind yourself of the first poem in *The Whitsun Weddings*, 'Here'. To what extent do you agree with the view that, in terms of subject matter and style, this poem is an appropriate introduction to the collection?

7 A modern poet has described 'P. Larkin and that lot' as 'not exactly a laugh a minute, pretty gloomy really'. Is this a fair assessment of this collection of poems?

8 Remind yourself of the last poem in *The Whitsun Weddings*, 'An Arundel Tomb'. To what extent do you agree with the view that, in terms of subject matter and style, this poem is an appropriate ending to the whole collection?

9 How far do you agree with the view that 'Larkin's presentation of relationships between men and women is always pessimistic'? In your answer you should EITHER refer to TWO or THREE poems OR range more widely through the collection.

10 How far do you agree that 'Larkin views advertising and consumerism with disapproval'? In your answer you should EITHER refer to TWO or THREE poems OR range more widely through the collection.

11 'The poems set up a conflict between a person's desires and the realities of life.' Using 'Mr Bleaney' as a starting point, and referring to AT LEAST TWO other poems, consider how useful you find this comment in studying Larkin's poetry.

12 Larkin himself said: 'I should hate people to read my work because they've been told to and told what to think about it. I really want the readers to feel *yes, I've never thought of it that way, but that's how it is.*' Explore the impact of Larkin's poetry in the light of his hopes about his readers. Refer to AT LEAST THREE poems in your answer.

13 'Larkin's poetry often starts on the solid commonplace world of the twentieth century but ends in the abstract and the uncertain.' Using in your answer an examination of 'Ambulances' and AT LEAST TWO other poems, explore this reading of Larkin's poetry.

14 'Larkin's poetry frequently expresses a tension between his justification of isolation and longing for community.' How far do you agree? You should base your answer on an examination of AT LEAST THREE poems.

15 **'Larkin is often thought of as a gloomy poet, describing the world around him in a drab and depressing way. Yet this is only one half of Larkin.' Explore this idea, using the poem 'The Whitsun Weddings' as a starting point and examining AT LEAST TWO other poems.**

16 **'Poetry has been described as "a fresh look and a fresh listen". Larkin's work fits this description: it challenges what society normally takes for granted.' Examine AT LEAST THREE poems in the light of this claim.**

17 **'Many of Larkin's poems reveal a powerful sense of remoteness from the world in which he lives.' How far do you agree? You should base your answer on an examination of 'The Importance of Elsewhere' and AT LEAST TWO other appropriate poems of your choice.**

18 **'What Larkin's poetry reflects is not so much class snobbery as a distaste for all things synthetic.' To what extent does this fit with your reading of the poems? You should base your answer on an examination of THREE OR MORE appropriate poems of your choice.**

19 **A critic has argued that Larkin reveals in his poetry an impoverished view of human possibilities. How far do you agree? You should include in your answer an examination of 'Dockery and Son' as well as AT LEAST TWO other poems.**

20 **'Larkin preserved a distance between himself and others; he said that he felt an intense need to be on the outside edge of things.' In the light of this statement, explore Larkin's poetic treatment of 'distance'. In your answer you should refer to AT LEAST THREE poems.**

Sample essays

Below are two sample student essays, both falling within the top mark band. You can judge them against the Assessment Objectives for this text for your exam board and decide on the mark you think each deserves, and why. You will be able to see ways in which each could be improved in terms of content, style and accuracy.

I would like to thank the students and staff of Wellington College, Berkshire, for permission to use these essays in this publication.

Sample essay 1

How far do you agree that Larkin's presentation of love reflects his fundamentally pessimistic view of life? Consider this view with reference to a selection of poems from *The Whitsun Weddings*.

Larkin stated that 'a good poem about failure is a success'. Although in 'An Arundel Tomb', 'Afternoons', 'The Whitsun Weddings' and 'Wild Oats' Larkin universally adopts a pessimistic view of time souring the transient myth of love, each poem also uniquely defends the power, beauty, mystery and desire of love. In all these poems Larkin describes the failure of love. However, it is in his acknowledgement of the basic desire and need for love despite its false pretensions that we can identify his success. The paradoxical alignment of love's untruth and its beauty allow Larkin to write successfully about the failure of love to materialise and last, but also to comment on humanity's need to believe in love.

All four poems reflect Larkin's pessimistic view of love. The equivocal and paradoxical idea, which Larkin often adopts, of love as having a transient yet cyclical nature is central to his cynicism regarding the subject. In 'Afternoons' Larkin writes about the cycle of love. From the beginning of the poem, however, the reader is presented with the analogy of domestic life being like autumn; the hope and myth of promised romance celebrated in 'The Whitsun Weddings' is over and the inevitable decay of a 'hollow' domestic life and routine have begun; 'Summer is fading:/The leaves fall in ones and twos'. 'Afternoons' reinforces Larkin's view of marriage as a social expectation that sours the hope of love. The mundane state of marriage is seen when he comments:

An estateful of washing,
And the albums, lettered
Our Wedding, lying
Near the television

The way in which the wedding album, which symbolises the climax of the youthful, romantic marriage, is discarded among the empty matter of the home shows the meaningless superficiality of the event; the honeymoon is over – the reality of married life corrupts and destroys the myth. The pun on 'lying' suggests the stillness, inactivity and apathy, but also underlines the ultimately deceptive nature of the relationship into which the couple has entered.

The central metaphor Larkin employs in 'An Arundel Tomb' again draws on stillness; the static, dignified, beautiful carving of the tomb and its passage through time appears to show the transcendent power of love. However, Larkin subtly undermines this view and uses the vagueness and ambiguity of the ultimately inconclusive metaphor to suggest the emptiness of mankind's romantic notion that love can transcend time; it is a momentary hope, a misinterpreted myth represented in the tomb. Larkin describes the way in which, unusually, the earl and countess lie side by side holding hands, 'His hand withdrawn, holding her hand'. This supposed symbol of love and devotion, however, is eroded by Larkin's cold description of the carving as merely a sculptor's 'sweet commissioned grace'. He also describes the faces of the carving as blurred, further detracting from the sense of meaningful definition. The facelessness of the couple leads to a sense of impersonality, a life withered rather than resilient to age – love appears as a victim of time. The word 'blurred' also implies a lack of identity and meaning; the tomb is an unclear, distorted and imprecise representation of love and individuality within love.

The lack of individuality which the social expectation of love produces is highlighted by Larkin in 'The Whitsun Weddings'. This is a poem which appears to explore the celebration and promise of love. However, the picture is not straightforward. Larkin also presents the social conformity of marriage, cheapening it to a 'Success so huge and wholly farcical'. This is demonstrated as he parodies the guests at the weddings he passes, who cause him to re-evaluate what he sees:

> And saw it all again in different terms:
> The fathers with broad belts under their suits
> And seamy foreheads; mothers loud and fat;
> An uncle shouting smut; and then the perms,
> The nylon gloves and jewellery-substitutes

His description of each 'new and nondescript' wedding and the language he employs stresses the coarseness and vulgar superficiality of the celebrations.

In all of these poems there is a sense of Larkin's position as an outsider, uninvolved in the intensity of what he sees, retaining his detachment from society and its views, which allows him clarity of insight and vent for his cynicism.

In 'Wild Oats' Larkin employs ironic humour to explore the nature of romance. Again, his cynical views come to the fore when he refers to the courting process as a 'shooting-match', something dangerous but strangely fascinating. He uses the two women in the poem to establish the contrast between a fantasy desire ('A bosomy English rose') and the attainable reality ('her friend in specs'). The love the poem pursues is marked by its pragmatism and lack of romance. It is a cheap love, summed up in the 'ten-guinea ring' he gave but 'got back in the end'. The reader is made to feel the inevitable bathos of the situation as the sexual excursions to 'cathedral cities' and the engagement collapse into an ironic memory.

Larkin's view of love, however, is not without its beauty and mystery. In 'Afternoons' Larkin comments on the 'beauty' of the young mothers, a beauty which he tells us 'thickened' with time, as if it has become more robust and dignified. 'The Whitsun Weddings' ends with an anticipation of the future. The final lines of the poem may reflect a positive promise and hope:

> there swelled
> A sense of falling, like an arrow-shower
> Sent out of sight, somewhere becoming rain.

This may be taken to reinforce the beauty and intensity of love and a promising energy and fertility.

'An Arundel Tomb' provides another potentially promising and beautiful portrayal of love. The purity of natural images such as the snow and the sunlight which 'Each summer thronged the glass' create an undeniable positivity, reflecting the persistence of love through the ages. The 'endless' generations that come to see the tomb also suggests the enduring need humanity has of love.

Despite the focus on limiting domesticity in 'Afternoons', the illusion of love in 'Wild Oats', the ultimate inability of love to endure in 'An Arundel Tomb' and the apparently empty celebrations of marriage in 'The Whitsun Weddings', Larkin is never unambiguous on the subject of love. 'An Arundel Tomb', in recognising 'our almost-instinct almost true', cannot (and does not seek to) deny the importance of love; on the contrary it proves this need powerfully, even if it does prove ultimately illusory.

Sample essay 2

For Larkin in *The Whitsun Weddings*, the details of living are only 'a struggle to transcend the thought of dying'. Discuss with specific reference to TWO or THREE poems of your choice.

In *The Whitsun Weddings*, Larkin often confronts his own fears, anxieties and uncertainties concerning death. Larkin presents the routine and ordinary details of living as being a struggle and a distraction to transcend the thought of dying. His central anxiety is that the domestic and mundane details of life may be all that survive of us; that 'how we live measures our own nature'. Larkin's fear and uncertainty about the complexities of mortality are expressed in 'Days', where the meaningless round of days is brought into sharp focus by the approach of the doctor and the priest. In 'Ambulances', Larkin portrays the details of living as merely a temporary distraction, vulnerable to the inevitability of death. However, despite Larkin's fearful and pessimistic portrayal of death, in 'An Arundel Tomb' he presents hope, resilience and a sense of strange beauty in death. This is especially evident in the enduring final words of the poem: 'what will survive of us is love.'

In 'Days', Larkin creates a contrast and tension between the simple, direct register of the poem's language and the difficult, undefined and complex reality of death, its key theme. The direct simplicity of the language is reflected in the build-up of monosyllables in the first stanza. Larkin also employs questions, reminiscent of a child's, to further establish a feeling of tension. While apparently straightforward, these questions are profoundly problematic, making the reader increasingly aware of a deep sense of uncertainty and unknowing. 'What are days for?' the poem opens. The reader, however, is quickly alert to the true meaning of this question, which masks a metaphysical probing into the very nature of and reason for human existence. Such gaps between appearance and reality are evident throughout the poem, but become particularly evident in the final stanza where death is portrayed in a comforting, almost pastorally idyllic fashion:

> the priest and the doctor
> In their long coats
> Running over the fields.

This is an almost childlike euphemism for death, which foregrounds the bleak and lonely reality of dying and the end of days. Days, Larkin suggests, are merely time meaninglessly preoccupied before the inevitability of death: 'They come, they wake us/Time and time over.' The mundane, predictable and inescapable cycle of living is reflected in the knowing certainty of Larkin's language, and only death provides a way out of this routine. 'Days' exemplifies Larkin's own fears outlining the central anxiety that living is meaningless and that time is no more than a thin and vulnerable barrier that separates us from death.

In 'Ambulances', Larkin presents the details of living as a temporary distraction that is prey to the inevitability of death. The image of the ambulance 'threading' its way through a city to a critical event causes Larkin to confront the issue of mortality – it becomes a symbol of death in the midst of life. The ambulances he envisions are 'Closed like confessionals', making illness and death seem secretive, disturbing and uncertain. The religious overtones of the word 'confessionals' – the confessional is a place of secrecy – are also significant, seeming to suggest that illness and death are like a sin that needs to be admitted and somehow purged. The fact that they are described as 'threading' their way through the streets is also important. This suggests, as in 'Days', that death is woven into life, an inescapable and natural part of the process of living. The ambulances are, however, a frightening presence. They appear fast and hostile, 'giving back/None of the glances they absorb'; they are impenetrable and fearsome, and have the power to appear anywhere: 'They come to rest at any kerb' – all are open to the arrival of the ambulances and what they signify.

Throughout the poem Larkin suggests the impossibility of true detachment from the thought of death. Once death has revealed itself it makes life irrelevant in the face of the certainty that 'All streets in time are visited'. The routines of daily life appear as attempts to distract from the inevitability of what must come, deflections from the fearful truth that faces everyone. However, such distractions are shattered upon the arrival of the ambulances:

> The fastened doors recede. *Poor soul,*
> They whisper at their own distress

The employment of the word 'soul', with its spiritual overtones, reminds us of the earlier 'confessionals', setting the poem in an eternal context, but it is striking that the true fear is not altruistically formed into sympathy for the sufferer, rather it reflects selfishly back on to the watchers, who are filled with fear of their own mortality. This selfish fear is, Larkin suggests, the motivation for the round of daily life. The lives of the men, women and children in the streets are protected from 'the solving emptiness/That lies just under all we do' by the demands of work (see also 'Toads Revisited'), domestic chores and play that distract their attention from such unendurable realities. It is clear, however, that such distractions can never win the 'struggle to transcend the thought of dying'. Towards the end of the poem Larkin presents a scene of dissolution as 'the unique random blend/ Of families and fashions' unravel and 'loosen'. The inevitability of death that he portrays means that the details of living will never overcome it, they are transitory, forgotten and 'dull to distance'.

Despite Larkin's pessimistic views on the inevitability of mortality, in 'An Arundel Tomb' he presents the possibility of beauty, resilience and, most importantly, hope in death. The central metaphor of the tomb's movement through time appears to show the vagueness and emptiness of death as well as the transitory nature of life – that all that will survive of us are hollow memorials. His language, however, undermines this view. The poem, more poignantly, illustrates the instinctive desire and need for humanity to believe in the hope of enduring love and that something will survive of us after death. Larkin portrays the tomb and the statues that lie on top of it as a symbol of love by describing the way in which the earl and countess lie side by side, 'His hand withdrawn, holding her hand'. The tomb's survival across the centuries ('Snow fell, undated') demonstrates the ability of love to endure. The purity and beauty of this image reflects the persistence of love through time. The pilgrimage of 'endless' generations speaks of the powerful and ongoing hope that this carries for humanity. In the apparent image of death the statues represent, Larkin finds a symbol of beauty and mystery. The carving lies:

> helpless in the hollow of
> An unarmorial age, a trough
> Of smoke in slow suspended skeins

This image juxtaposes the concrete (the trough) with the abstract (the smoke), creating an air of mystery, and setting out the impossibility of defining the true nature of what has survived of this couple, and how. Like the drifting mist, the faces of the carving are vague; eroded by time, they are blurred, elusive and ephemeral. This may indicate the passing nature of romance, but keeps alive the vague, mist-like hope that something endures after death – the beautiful, mysterious and not unambiguous 'attitude' that is love. Even in the midst of this 'Bone-riddled ground' there is a sense of the eternal. Most importantly, 'An Arundel Tomb' keeps alive the possibility that there is more to life than mere daily routine. The qualified final line is as near as Larkin comes to affirmation as it proves 'Our almost-instinct almost true:/What will survive of us is love'. Self-deception it may ultimately be, but this conclusion dignifies and retains the importance of such self-deceptions.

In *The Whitsun Weddings*, Larkin often addresses his own fears and anxieties concerning mortality. He presents the routines and ordinary details of life as being a struggle to keep death at bay and a distraction to transcend the thought of dying, as in 'Days' and 'Ambulances'. Death is an inevitable and ubiquitous force throughout the collection. However, in the final poem of the collection, 'An Arundel Tomb', the reader is left at least with the hope that something may be more powerful than death.

Using the critics

The role of literary criticism and literary theory in the study of literature at both AS and A2 is central. Assessment Objective 4 specifically requires students to 'articulate informed, independent judgements, showing understanding of different interpretations of literary texts by different readers'.

While this does not necessarily mean that all such interpretations should be by established literary critics or propound particular theoretical readings, the implication that these should be covered as part of advanced study is clear, especially where incisive and detailed analysis is required. Furthermore, the emphasis placed on a range of readings makes the use of criticism essential to success.

The following is an extract from the AQA specification, developing some of the implications of Assessment Objective 4:

> Candidates will be expected to show awareness of the following:
>
> - that, as readers, we are influenced by our own experiences, actual or imagined, and that our cultural background has an effect on our interpretation; thus the interpretation of literary texts, or the determination of their significance, can depend on the interpretative stance taken by the reader
> - that there might be significant differences in the way literary texts are understood in different periods, and by different individuals or social groups
> - that texts do not reflect an external and objective reality; instead they embody attitudes and values
> - that there are different ways of looking at texts, based on particular approaches and theories. Using these theories will require some understanding of critical concepts and terminology
> - that literary texts are frequently open-ended, so ambiguity and uncertainty are central to the reading of texts. Examination tasks will therefore expect candidates to take part in genuine critical enquiry rather than respond to tasks where the teacher/examiner already knows the 'right' answer

You need to think carefully about how critical material should be used. The emphasis in examination specifications is firmly placed upon a candidate's ability to recognise and evaluate the validity of interpretations from a multiplicity of viewpoints. Approaching a text from a single critical perspective, therefore, or prioritising one at the expense of others, is neither desirable nor helpful. Successful students will apply and develop their critical thinking about the set text in the light of a variety of secondary critical texts.

It is essential, however, that students should not see the use of critical quotation as a virtue in its own right. Unthinking application of critical material is at best redundant and at worst prevents students from thinking for themselves. The key to

successful application of literary criticism and literary theory is to use it as a basis for argument. There are three basic positions that can be adopted:

(1) To agree with a critical proposition and to use this to support an argument or part of an argument.

(2) To agree with a proposition but with qualifications; identify clearly the areas of agreement, but go on to develop areas of disagreement, qualification, modification or extension of the ideas.

(3) To disagree with a proposition, explaining why.

All of these stances can, of course, be developed by going on to propose alternative critical or theoretical possibilities and evaluating the validity of one critical perspective over another in relation to the text or passage under consideration. To extend and enrich a response, the criticism used must be engaged with. The words of literary critics and literary theorists should not be taken as received wisdom to be applied unthinkingly to the text. Instead, you need to identify clearly the issues raised by the critic and then evaluate and test these in relation to the set text, which should always remain the primary focus of your response.

References and further study

Larkin's main works

Poetry

The North Ship (1945)
XX Poems (1951)
The Fantasy Poets No. 21 (1954)
Poems (1954)
The Less Deceived (1955)
The Whitsun Weddings (1964)
High Windows (1974)
Collected Poems 1938–1983 (1988)

Fiction

Jill (1946)
A Girl in Winter (1947)
Trouble at Willow Gables and Other Fictions (2002)

Non-fiction

Larkin, P. (1970) *All What Jazz: A Record Diary 1961–1971*, Faber & Faber
Larkin, P. (1983) *Required Writing: Miscellaneous Pieces 1955–1982*, Faber & Faber
Palmer, R. and White, J. (eds) (2001) *Larkin's Jazz: Essays and Reviews*, Continuum
Thwaite, A. (ed.) (1982) *Larkin at Sixty*, Faber & Faber

Thwaite, A. (ed.) (1992) *Selected Letters of Philip Larkin*, Faber & Faber
Thwaite, A. (ed.) (2001) *Further Requirements: Interviews, Broadcasts, Statements and Reviews, 1952–85,* Faber & Faber.

Biography

Motion, A. (1993) *Philip Larkin: A Writer's Life*, Faber & Faber

Literary criticism

Morrison, B. (1980) *The Movement: English Poetry and Fiction of the 1950s*, Oxford University Press
Rossen, J. (1989) *Philip Larkin: His Life's Work*, Harvester Wheatsheaf
Swarbrick, A. (1995) *Out of Reach: The Poetry of Philip Larkin*, Macmillan
Thwaite, A. (1970) 'The Poetry of Philip Larkin' in *The Survival of Poetry: A Contemporary Survey*, ed. M. Dodsworth, Faber & Faber

Websites

www.literaryhistory.com/20thC/Larkin.htm
www.philiplarkin.com
www.poets.org/poets/poets.cfm?prmID=179
www.todayinliterature.com/biography/philip.larkin.asp
www.infoplease.com/ce6/people/A0828895.html
www.litencyc.com/php/speople.php?rec=true&UID=2624

WITHDRAWN